# The Malay Art
## of Self-Defense

# The Malay Art of Self-Defense

## Silat Seni Gayong

**Sheikh Shamsuddin**

North Atlantic Books
*Berkeley, California*

Published by
North Atlantic Books
P.O. Box 12327
Berkeley, California 94712

Cover and text design by Brad Greene
Printed in the United States of America
Distributed to the book trade
by Publishers Group West

*The Malay Art of Self-Defense: Silat Seni Gayong* is sponsored by the Society for the Study of Native Arts and Sciences, a nonprofit educational corporation whose goals are to develop an educational and crosscultural perspective linking various scientific, social, and artistic fields; to nurture a holistic view of arts, sciences, humanities, and healing; and to publish and distribute literature on the relationship of mind, body, and nature.

North Atlantic Books' publications are available through most bookstores. For further information, call 800-337-2665 or visit our website at www.northatlanticbooks.com.

Substantial discounts on bulk quantities are available to corporations, professional associations, and other organizations. For details and discount information, contact our special sales department.

Library of Congress Cataloging-in-Publication Data

Shamsuddin, Sheikh.
  The Malay art of self-defense : silat seni gayong / by Sheikh Shamsuddin.
    p. cm.
  ISBN 1-55643-562-2 (pbk.)
  1. Self-defense. 2. Hand-to-hand fighting. 3. Pencak silat. I. Title.
  GV1111.S385 2005
  613.6'6--dc22
                                        2005011984

1 2 3 4 5 6 7 8 9 DATA 10 09 08 07 06 05

This book is dedicated to the late *mahaguru* of *silat seni gayong Dato* Meor Abdul Rahman, his family, and to all *anak anak gayong* (*gayong* practitioners) worldwide. Gayong Malaysia, Gayong Pusaka, Gayong Warisan, and Gayong PASAK we are one *silat*—*silat seni gayong.*

*Dato* **Meor Abdul Rahman, the founder of** *silat seni gayong.*

# Disclaimer

Even though both the publisher and the author of this book have taken enormous care to verify the authenticity of the information and techniques or movements enclosed herein, we do not guarantee or assume any responsibility for how the information is interpreted or used. The nature of martial arts training makes injuries possible. It is crucial that extreme caution be exercised at all times when practicing. Readers are advised to consult their physician before engaging in any of these activities. Readers are solely responsible for any liabilities that may occur as a result of their actions.

Readers are reminded that federal, state, and local laws may prohibit the use of weapons described in this book. A detailed examination must be made of federal, state, and local laws before the reader attempts to use these weapons in self-defense situations. We do not guarantee the legality or the appropriateness of the techniques, movements, or weapons discussed herein.

# Contents

# Foreword

The mission of the International Pencak Silat Federation, Pentjak Silat USA™ is to promote the health benefits, ideals, art, science, and philosophy of *pencak silat* to its members and community.

In response to the rising popularity of *pencak silat* among martial arts aficionados, *Ketua Khalifah* Sheikh Shamsuddin brings the history and traditions of this exotic art form to the Western world. With the help of Shamsuddin, *pencak silat seni gayong* continues to promote quality, honor, as well as respect for community and self in *pencak* the United States. These qualities are exemplified in the International Pencak Silat Federation, Pentjak Silat USA™ of which he and his fine organization are members. Shamsuddin's efforts and the publishing of this book qualify him as another pioneer of *pencak silat*. He continues in the tradition of the earlier greats such as: Willem Reeders, Willie Wetzel, the De Thouars family, Rudy ter Linden, James Ingram, and Dan Inosanto. It is through the strength of such individuals and the ongoing efforts of our organizations that genuine and authentic *pencak silat* has gained a solid foothold in the United States and will continue to flourish.

—Professor André KnustGraichen, CEO,
International Pencak Silat Federation, Pentjak Silat USA™
Founded and Est. 1990
Incorporated in the State of California 1993
as 501(3)(c) non-profit organization

# Preface

The idea of writing this book has intrigued me for several years. I kept trying to put it aside, but to no avail. The inquisitive minds of my dedicated and enthusiastic students kept forming questions for me regarding the Malay *silat,* particularly *gayong silat.* There are numerous *gayong* references on the Internet, but most of them are written in Malay. I have tried to listen to my students' needs, questions, problems, and suggestions sensitively to determine what would be helpful to them. I decided to write this book for their education and my love of the art. I hope it will guide *gayong* students worldwide.

To the best of my knowledge, this is the first *gayong* book ever written in the United States. This is another reason I felt compelled to write it—so that the truth about the art, culture, and tradition is preserved. It is my hope that with this book all *gayong* students and instructors are well informed and prepared to share the art without corrupting it. I sincerely hope that this book will inspire other practitioners to write more about *gayong* so that they can contribute to and uncover the hidden treasures that *gayong* has to offer.

Writing this book was not an easy task for me because there were numerous essential topics that needed to be covered. I had to be selective about which subjects to introduce without complicating the material. I wanted to make the material informative and precise without it being overly complicated or losing any of the true meaning.

I genuinely hope that readers interpret the book with open minds and a positive manner. And I also hope that it serves as an introduction to *gayong* to those who are new to the art. I am presenting my knowledge of *gayong* defense and concepts as a solid foundation upon which to build. The techniques included are basic, derived from several *asas elakkan* (block movement maneuvering) and variations of *gayong* techniques called *pecahan* on super combat and *pukulan*. It is impossible to introduce all of the *gayong* techniques. They are flexible and can adapt to all kinds of attacks. The possibilities are limitless.

*Seni gayong silat* is not my art. It is an art that belongs to and is inherited by the Malay people. I am merely a practitioner and intend to share my knowledge with those who want to discover it.

The intention of this book is to introduce *silat* in general and *silat seni gayong* in particular. The first part of the book presents an overview of *silat* and its history. Then *gayong*'s history and founder are detailed. A glimpse of *gayong* hierarchy is presented so that readers will understand the evolution or rather revolution that took place from the early period until present. A section about the connotation of *gayong,* its philosophy and the *adat* (culture and tradition) is also included. Because in every *silat* style the *keris* (dagger) is a part of the art's system, a brief *keris* section is included. *Gayong* curriculum is included and *gayong* forms are selectively presented in step-by-step pictures. This will show readers what *gayong* techniques look like. There is a commonly asked questions and answers section. Because *silat* is an art predominantly practiced by people in Southeast Asia, a section about American perspectives is included. At the end of the book, classical names of *gayong* styles are included as a reference. The famous story of two Malay warriors, Hang Tuah and Hang Jebat, is also included to give insight into how *silat* and *adat* are related to the story. Because *gayong* is native to Malaysia, a tour of the country is provided. A short section of language translation is also included for those who are curious about the *Bahasa* Malaysia. Finally, there are collected pictures of *gayong* activities.

I would like to express my personal appreciation to all of my colleagues who have encouraged me to write this book. I would also like to thank all of the martial arts instructors that I have studied under throughout my life. Each and every one of them has taught me valuable lessons about self-defense and life. They include:

- *Gayong silat Mahaguru Dato* Meor Abdul Rahman

- *Cikgu* Majid Mat Isa

- *Cikgu* Awang Daud

- *Cikgu* Siti Kalsom

- *Cikgu* Safiah Mohd Noor

- *Cikgu* Sani Morni

- *Cikgu* Kahar Redza

- *Cikgu* Azhar Abbas

- *Cikgu* Adiwijaya

- *Cikgu* Razali Salleh

- *Cikgu* Zainal Ishak

- *Aikido* instructors Judith Leppert *Sensei* and her assistants Matthias Lynch *Sensei,* Bernard Calma *Sensei,* and Graig Neville *Sensei*

- *Hapkido* instructors master Hyun Bae You and master Randy Stigall

- *Kosho ryu kempo* comrade Bruce Juchnik Hanshi

- *Kuntao silat* comrade Guru William De Thouars and Guru André KnustGraichen

- *Serak silat* comrade Guru Victor De Thouars

- *Mustika kwitang silat* comrade Guru Jim Ingram

- *Taijiquan* comrade Sifu David Champ

**Sheikh Shamsuddin—Sam**

I also want to express my respect to all former and present *gayong* teachers.

Last but not least, I would like to thank all *gayong silat* organizations for trusting and believing in me to proliferate the treasures of *silat*. No matter what name *gayong* organizations propagate under, whether Gayong Malaysia, Gayong Pusaka, Gayong Warisan, or Gayong PASAK Singapore, it is still the precious art of *silat—silat seni gayong.*

I give respect to you all.

# Acknowledgments

Various people have supported and contributed to the successful creation of this book. I am grateful to these wonderful people for their willingness to take time from their busy lives to help me. I want to express my sincere appreciation to them.

Thank you to North Atlantic Books/Frog, Ltd. project editors Emily Boyd and Jess O'Brien, and to team members Paula Morrison, Kristan Ruona, and Brad Greene for working so closely with me.

Thank you to Marcy Slane and Melvin Slane for proofreading my manuscript.

Azlan Ghanie, the executive director and owner of the Malaysian *silat* magazine *Seni Beladiri* in Kuala Lumpur for giving me authorization to use pictures from his magazines and for giving me his complete support and cooperation.

Thank you Tourism Malaysia Organization in New York for giving me permission to use images of Malaysian scenery and local culture.

Onn Jadi, a Malaysian *gayong* student from the Association of Silat Seni Gayong Malaysia at the University of Malaya Campus in Kuala Lumpur, for allowing me to use *gayong* pictures and images from his Web site and for sharing past and present *gayong* information.

Thank you to my students Joel Champ, Joshua Champ, Jennifer Para, Neel Tummala, and Daniel Snyder, for helping me take pictures for the techniques and for allowing me to abuse, throw, kick, twist, slam, and smack them.

Thank you to Jon Ludwig *Sensei* (*khoso ryu kempo* instructor) for his support of *gayong* activities and for his contribution to the design of the book cover and other *gayong* images. I thank him for his kindness for allowing us to share his training institute.

Thank you to my *gayong* colleagues in Malaysia for giving me guidance and sharing their experiences and information about the *gayong* organization and activities in Malaysia. They are: Sani Morni, Anuar Hamid, Rasol Abdul Ghanie, Faid Musa, Zainal Ishak, Kahar Redza, Azhar Abbas, and the two Gayong Malaysia secretaries, Siti Zubaidah Kamaruzaman and Noraishah Shawaluddin.

Thank you to Ariffin Mahidin from *gayong* United Kingdom, for giving me support and sharing information.

Many of the *silat* pictures within this book are courtesy of Malaysian *gayong* Web sites. Some are courtesy of *Cikgu* Sani Morni, Onn Jadi, *Seni Beladiri* magazine, and *Cikgu* Ariffin from the United Kingdom. I thank you all for your contributions.

Thank you to my lovely wife Melanie for editing my original manuscript and for helping me with the English language. Lastly, thank you to my beautiful daughters, Leila and Jasmine, for their typing skills and unending support.

The author *Cikgu* Sam and *Cikgu* Joel Champ

CHAPTER 1

# What Is Silat?

*Silat* is the combative art of fighting and survival believed to have originated from ancient
Malaysian and Indonesian civilizations. Until
recently there has been no fixed form of instruc-
tion. It has now evolved to become part of
social culture and tradition and is a fine physical
and spiritual training. There are various styles
of *silat*. *Silat burung putih* is based on bird-style
fighting. *Silat tjmande* is water-buffalo-style fighting. *Silat tjikalong* is crane-style fighting. *Silat
harimau* is based on tiger-style fighting. Not all
*silats* are fighting arts; some are merely danc-
ing forms such as *silat pulut*.

*Sangga maut* **technique**

The definition of the word *silat* varies from one *guru* or *cikgu*
(teacher) to another. The Malay dictionary defines *silat* as a *seni* (art)
with the intelligence to attack and defend gracefully. Another meaning states that *silat* originated from the word *kilat* (lightning). A practitioner tries to acquire the characteristics of lightning: speed,
dominance, sharpness, fluidity, and danger. A person with these qualities and intelligence was called *sikilat*. The word eventually came to
be pronounced *silat*. Another meaning states that the word *silat* orig-

inates from the Arabic language. If the word *silat* is spelled with the Arabic letter *seen*, the word *silat* means *brotherhood*. If the word is spelled with the Arabic letter s*aad*, it means weapons. Some believe that the word *silat* originated from the Malay word *silap* or *solat*. *Solat* means to pray or concentrate, to communicate among mankind and the creator. *Silap* means imprecision; the hidden concept of defending oneself by making intentional mistakes while seeking and sensing the adversary's open movements *(langkah silap dan langkah sumbang)* to abort the physical attack. Another definition defines *silat* as the Malay art and science of armed and unarmed combat. Yet another meaning of *silat* is simply "to ward off."

In Indonesia, the art is commonly referred to as *pentjak silat*. *Pentjak silat*, also spelled *pencak silat*, means to defend oneself. In Malaysia, the words *silat* or *seni silat* are frequently used rather than *pencak silat*. *Seni* means art. It is internal, delicate, wise, and elegant. It is a substance that one cannot comprehend by theorizing it, but rather by sensing it. *Seni silat* is analogous to spiritual and physical well being. *Bersilat* is a verb. It means, "to do *silat*." In view of the fact that *silat* has some Indian and Chinese influence, some believe that the word *pentjak* might be derived from a Chinese word *pen-cha* (avert or deflect) and the word *silat* from the Chinese word *sau-la* (push hands or to perform with the hands).

There are a variety of *silat* styles. In Malaysia alone there are more than 150 known *silat* styles. Some of the known styles found in Malaysia are:

- *Gayong*
- *Melayu*
- *Cekak*
- *Bunga*
- *Pulut*
- *Kelantan*

*Pasak mati* technique.

- *Lincah*
- *Kalimah*
- *Rajawali*
- *Burung Puteh*
- *Gayong Fatani*

- *Gayong Ghaib*
- *Sendeng*
- *Gerak Kilat*
- *Silat Melayu Keris Lok 9*

Examples of Indonesian *silat* are:

- *Tapak Suji*
- *Tjikalong*
- *Lintow*
- *Setia Hati*
- *Kuntao*
- *Perisai Diri*
- *Bahkti Negara*

- *Tjimande*
- *Serak*
- *Perisai Sahkti*
- *Menangkabau*
- *Delima*
- *Jawa*

Some *silats* are performed with Malay drums or other musical instruments while more vigorous and less rhythmic *silats* are not. Whichever *silat* style you learn, each is unique and stands on its very own. To assume that they are all similar is oversimplification.

In general, *silat* techniques use hand and foot maneuverings. The principle of *silat* is to evade attack. Training in *silat* includes cultural, spiritual, and mental aspects as well as tumbling, striking, kicking, blocking, and agility movements. Many movements are described by names. Some are poetic, some are named after an animal's movement, and some are metaphors. Here are examples:

**Typical silat musical instruments.**

*Serangan Harimau*—Tiger Attack

*Kacip Emas*—Golden Slicer

*Tarian Kuda Gila*—Crazy Horse Dance

*Tali Gantong*—Hanging Rope

*Ular Sawa Berendam*—Sinking Python

*Timang Puteri*—Winding Princess

*Patah Dayong Nasi Hangit*—Broken Paddle Overcooked Rice

*Malaikat Maut*—Angel of Death

*Silat* is a Malay symbol of identity as in *taekwondo* for Korea and *aikido* for Japan. However, *silat* is understood to be a creation by an ethnic Malay group rather than an art coming from a specific country. The characteristics that make *silat* distinctive from other martial arts include its use of:

- The culture and tradition of the Malay ethnic group as its source and model.

- Mental-spiritual, artistic, graceful, and flowery movements similar to Malay classical dance paired with seemingly incompatible martial aspects.

- Looking slantingly to the ground and sensing the adversary's movements rather than using direct eye contact. In some instances the practitioners seem to be in a trance-like state and possess an eerie ability to anticipate the opponent's movements.

CHAPTER 2

# Brief History of Silat

The exact origin of *silat* is uncertain. However, there is evidence of both cultural and combative influences from other countries such as India and China. Martial art authors Donn F. Draeger and Qiutin Chambers acknowledge the fact that *silat* is a genuine Malay art in the book *Javanese Silat: The Fighting of Perisai Diri*. Malays are the people who inhabit the Malay peninsula (Peninsular Malaysia) and parts of adjacent islands of Southeast Asia including Indonesia, Borneo, and Singapore. Malays, particularly in Peninsular Malaysia, consider the legendary warrior Laksamana Hang Tuah (Admiral Hang Tuah) of the fourteenth century to be the father of *silat*.

There are various theories and speculation about the origin of *silat*. Nevertheless, none have profound evidence of support. Because there are many types and styles of *silat,* there is no one founder of this type of self-defense. Concrete proof describing the development of various *silat* styles is difficult to find. History denotes that *silat* existed as far back as the seventh century A.D. Most likely during that time the defense forms were still in the infancy stage. It was not until fourteenth-century empires such as the Malacca, the Majapahit and the Srivijaya that *silat* was refined and became the specialized property of the sultans and their *Panglima* and *Pendekar* (warriors). At that time, places such as the Malay peninsula, Bali, Java, the Sulawisi, and Bor-

neo island were all under the influence of these fourteenth-century empires. Later, as empires were weakened by civil wars, *silat* began to spread slowly throughout Southeast Asia, from Java to Sumatra, to the Malay peninsula, to Sulawisi island, to Borneo island, to the Philippines, and to other areas within the Southeast Asian continent.

When the people living in the region were under the authority of foreign colonial powers such as the British, Dutch, Portuguese, and Japanese, *silat* was regarded as a means to cultivate national spirit and was strictly prohibited. Because anyone caught practicing *silat* was severely punished, *silat* activities were continued in secrecy.

After the people of the region had been liberated from foreign authorities, the growth of *silat* spread rapidly. Several countries within the region began to standardize *silat* by forming a national organization. In Malaysia, the Persatuan Silat Kebangsaan Malaysia (PESAKA) (Malaysian National Silat Federation) was formed. In Indonesia, the Ikatan Pencak Silat Indonesia (IPSI) (Indonesian Pencak Silat Association) was formed. In Singapore, the Persatuan Silat Singapore (PERSIS) (Singaporean Silat Federation) was formed. In Brunei, the Persatuan Silat Brunei Darussalam (PERSIB) (Brunei Darussalam Silat Federation) was formed. Today, *silat* has emerged as a national standard and has spread into Europe and the western world. In the United States, an International Pencak Silat Federation (IPSF) has been formed to promote *silat*. In Europe the Silat Association of the United Kingdom was formed.

More information about the history of *silat* can be found in *The Weapons and Fighting Arts of Indonesia* written by Donn F. Draeger.

# CHAPTER 3

# Silat Gayong

*Silat gayong* is an art of self-defense. It is a defensive art, an art for stopping wars not creating them. *Gayong* is not merely about self-defense; it is also a way to develop the self—*belajar mengenal diri* (becoming a better person so that one may serve humanity). Gayong is a tool to strengthen relationships among mankind. It is a great way to develop and to increase physical fitness, flexibility, mental conditioning, discipline, and self-confidence. The philosophy of *gayong* is strongly related to the *Malay adat istiadat* (Malay cultures and traditions), morals, *adab* (respect), and the teaching of religion. Religion is the inspiration, motivation, and guidance for high-quality behavior. It is a mark of peace and harmony.

At one time, *gayong* was taught only to select people. It was not until early 1942 when, on the Sudong island village of Singapore, inhabitants were worried about an attack by the Japanese army and the secret of *gayong* became more widely known. The incident was the first step in making *gayong* available to the public. From the Sudong island, *gayong* spread to other vicinities such as the island of Seking, Bukum, Sebaruk,

**Figure 3-1: Dato Meor Abdul Rahman**

Sekijang, Sembilan, Semakom, and Damar island. It spread through-out the Indonesian islands as a way to protect the villages from pirates.

Today, *gayong* is widely practiced in Malaysia and Singapore. The art is being taught in schools, colleges, to the armed forces, and to the Royal Malaysian Police. It also plays an important role for younger generations. *Gayong* has become a way to educate and introduce good character, discipline, morals, and ethics. It inspires the youth of Malaysia to appreciate the legends of the nation, the culture and tradition, and the achievement of freedom and liberty.

*Gayong* has traveled beyond Malaysian society to Australia, Kuwait, Tunisia, Vietnam, France, Europe, and now to the United States.

**Figure 3-2: The author in the U.S.**

# CHAPTER 4

# History of Gayong

*Seni gayong silat,* or more correctly pronounced in the Malay language *silat seni gayong,* is believed to have originated from the Bugis tribe in the Sulawesi island (also known as Celebes island). The original name of *silat seni gayong* was *silat seni sendi harimau.* It is believed that *gayong* has existed since the era of the Malacca's sultanate in the Malay Peninsula in the late fourteenth century during the empire of the Sultan Mansor Shah. In 1511, during the intervention of the Portuguese in Malacca, Tun Biajid, son of Laksamana Hang Tuah (figure 4-1), and his followers employed *silat* to protect the Malay empire and its people. *Gayong* continued to spread from one generation to the next, and later to the grandfather of Meor Rahman, Syed Zainal Al-Attas, who lived in the era of *Pendakar Dato* Bahaman and Mat Kilau in 1700. Malaysians considered *Dato* Bahaman and Mat Kilau as freedom fighters during the British occupation of Malaysia. At that time, mostly the Bugis people of *Makasar* studied *gayong silat.* These were the people that brought *gayong* into the Malay Peninsula.

Figure 4-1

13

The *mahaguru* of *silat seni gayong* was *Dato* Meor Abdul Rahman. He was the descendent of Bugis and Arabs. His great grandfather, Prince Daeng Kuning (Daeng meaning prince of royal Bugis), was a famous warrior also known as *Panglima Hitam* (The Black Warrior). Daeng Kuning was recognized as a descendent of the family of warriors identified as *pahlawan gayong. Pahlawan gayong* was a famous warrior, highly intimidating, and respected by the public in Makasar, Riau, Siak, and all of the surrounding islands. History indicates that the Malay legendary warrior Hang Tuah inherited *gayong,* which was ultimately passed down to *Dato* Meor Abdul Rahman.

Daeng Kuning traveled from Sulawisi island to the Malay Peninsula sometime after the year 1800. He traveled with six of his close relatives. They were Daeng Jalak, Daeng Celak, Daeng Merawak, Daeng Mempawah, Daeng Telani, and Daeng Pelonggi. In search of a better life, they all went their separate ways throughout the Malay archipelago. Some moved to the state of Kedah, others to the states of Pahang, Johor, Terengganu, Selangor, and Malacca. Daeng Kuning settled in the state of Perak, married Princess Raja Patani, and decided to reside in the village of Air Kuning. They had a son named Penghulu Che Ngah Tambak who later had a son named Uda Mohd Hashim, the father of Meor Abdul Rahman. Daeng Kuning died in August 17, 1875 in Taiping, Perak. It is documented that *seni gayong* undoubtedly came from the lineage of the Bugis royal family:

Prince Daeng Kuning (The Black Warrior)

Penghulu Che Ngah Tambak

Daeng Uda Mohd Hashim

*Dato* Meor Abdul Rahman

The picture below shows *Dato* Meor Abdul Rahman's parents Daeng Uda Mohd Hashim and his wife Sharifah Aluyah, daughter of Syed Zainal Abidin Al-Attas.

**Figure 4-2:** *Dato* **Meor's parents**

# CHAPTER 5

# Dato Meor Abdul Rahman, the Mahaguru of Silat Seni Gayong— A Biography

Meor Abdul Rahman, son of Uda Mohd Hashim, was the originator and founder of *silat seni gayong.* He was born on August 17, 1915 in Taiping, Perak. (Perak is one of the thirteen states in Malaysia.) His mother was Syarifah Aluyah, daughter of Syed Zainal Al-Attas. He had a brother named Meor Aziz and a sister named Siti Syarifah. Before Meor Rahman was born, his mother had a dream that the child she was carrying would someday become a leader and warrior. Legend has it that Meor Rahman was born with an unformed twin, a little creature that looked like a worm. This worm-like creature was kept in a coconut shell for a while and then released into a river in Perak called Teluk Kertang. According to his mother, this was a sign that one day he would become a respected and well-known warrior.

In his early years, Meor Rahman received his education from a Malay school in the village of Pokok Asam in Taiping, and in his adolescent years he

**Figure 5-1: Meor teaching** *chindai* **movement**

attended King Edwards VII school, later joining a technical school until 1936.

Meor Rahman began learning *silat* when he was twelve years old from his grandfather on his mother's side, Syed Zainal Abidin Al-Attas, who inherited *gayong* from Daeng Ambok Solok a Bugis warrior residing in Jambi, Sumatra. When Meor Rahman was small, he heard many stories from his grandparents about legendary Malay warriors. He spent four solid years learning the *selok belok* (details) from his grandfather. Then his grandfather told him that he would finish his training some day in the southern border of Thailand with a mysterious being. After completing school, he spent most of his time visiting his brother-in-law who worked as a police officer in the area. There, he took the opportunity to expand his *silat* knowledge by learning from different *silat* gurus. However, his *silat* knowledge was much higher then the other gurus. Many *silat* masters challenged Meor, but none were equivalent to him.

Meor regularly went hunting for birds and wild roosters. One day he and his friends were hunting, and he wandered into the tropical forest near the southern Thailand border. He met an old man named Pak Choh who took him in as his adopted son. Knowing that Meor had a background as a warrior, he introduced him to Lim Choon. Lim arranged many competitions for Meor with several *Muay Thai* fighters. Because of Meor's excellent performance, he won many fights and was granted the title *pendekar* (warrior).

Meor finally reached a place called Mee Nam in southern Thailand and met a person he already knew, Tok Mekjah. It was at Mee Nam that the strange incident vaguely described by his grandfather happened. One day, feeling fatigued, he fell asleep on top of a giant black rock near the river. He dreamed of a mysterious being dressed as a traditional Malay warrior who approached him and introduced himself as the legendary Hang Tuah. (For more information read the *Who was Hang Tuah* section.) He instructed him to visit and pledge his loyalty to the Sultan of Perak. In his dream, Meor was given the essence and secrets of *silat* and when he woke he experienced strange sensations and possessed amazing strength. He later informed his parents of this occurrence and then offered to serve the Sultan of Perak, Sultan Alang Iskandar. Meor Rahman demonstrated his amazing skills and strength, and the sultan was greatly impressed and ultimately granted him the title *Rahman Sendo*, (the Invincible Warrior of Perak). Some of his strengths included bending a nine-inch nail with his bare hands, tug-of-war against multiple people, and folding a coin similar in size to a quarter. Meor Rahman became the adopted son of the sultan and lived with him until the sultan passed away in 1938.

**Figure 5-2: West Malaysia.**

While he was in Taiping, Meor taught *silat seni gayong* to some of his very close friends. His friends called him "Rahman, the Strong Man." At the same time, the sultan of the state of Kedah declared Meor Rahman the *Mahaguru*.

After the Sultan of Perak died, Meor Rahman moved to Singapore, then a Malaysian state, in search of a better life. He worked at several jobs and later served with the British Royal Signal Corp. at

Gillman Barracks, under the command of Lieutenant Colonial Pope. While there, a martial arts teacher challenged him to combat, and Meor Rahman was able to overcome him. He then became a combat instructor to coach the British Army in unarmed self-defense. He was the first Malay to hold such a position in the British government. When the Japanese attacked Singapore in 1942, Meor was instructed to relocate to the near-by Sudong island.

Before being allowed to reside on Sudong island, he was required to challenge *pendeker Wak Kusang* a group leader on the island. Meor successfully accomplished the task. In order to protect the inhabitants from being crushed by the Japanese army in early 1942, *gayong* was introduced to several chosen people. These people, along with the intelligence plan from Meor Rahman, secured the island. The Japanese army left the people of the island alone.

During the Japanese occupation of Malaysia in 1942, Meor Rahman was detained for resisting the Japanese troops and for injuring a Japanese soldier in order to protect his family. He was sentenced to death by hanging. In order to avoid the death sentence, he served in the Japanese army. In 1945 when the Japanese surrendered, Meor Rahman went back to Singapore where the Sudong island residents offered him work as *penghulu* (chief) of the village. He was chief of the village for two years and then joined the British government to work as a detective. In appreciation for his bravery in opposing the Japanese occupation on the island of Sudong, he was awarded the King George V Medal of Honor by the British government on December 23, 1947.

During Meor's stay on Sudong island, *silat seni gayong* began to proliferate from Sudong to Sembilan, Seking, Semulon, Bukum, Semantan, and all of the Indonesian islands surrounding the area

Figure 5-3: Meor surrounded by a dragon.

**Figure 5-4: Meor Rahman's brother.**

including Gerating and Terong. Sudong island became the center of *gayong*.

At the end of 1949, *gayong* was widely spread over Singapore and the Malay Peninsula. In the mid-1950s, many actors and actresses began to join *gayong*. In 1956, a very significant and respected Malay political figure, *Dato* Onn Jaffar, joined *gayong*. He was endorsed as the advisor of *silat seni gayong* traditions and culture.

In early 1957, Meor Rahman organized an exhibition of *silat* demonstrations in the state of Kedah. This was the first organized event, and the main objective was to propagate *gayong* to Malaysian society. In 1959, the first Institution of Gayong was established in Woodlands, Singapore. It was led by Meor Rahman. From this academy, more *gayong* instructors were produced.

In 1961, Meor Rahman retired from government work and started his own business. By then, *silat seni gayong* had spread throughout the Malay Peninsula. Meor Rahman was determined to bring more instructors to be supervised by he and his brother Meor Aziz to teach *gayong* at designated locations.

On October 22, 1963, *Dato* Onn Jaffar saw the possibility of forming an association to portray the art in its genuine state. This was the first *silat* ever recorded in Malaysia under the name *silat seni gayong* with the registered number 361. (The current registered number is APS 0149/98.) The headquarters was moved from Woodlands to Kota Sarang Semut in the state of Johor.

In 1964, a massive *gayong* exhibition was arranged in the northern Malay Peninsula. Due to the tremendous success of the demonstration, the Sultan of Kedah appointed Meor Rahman to teach *gayong* to the people of the state of Kedah. Many high-ranking elected officials in Malaysia began to practice *gayong*.

**Figure 5-5: Dato Onn Jaffar. A political leader.**

Toward the end of 1969, Meor Rahman moved back to Taiping. With assistance from some high-ranking *gayong* instructors, a *gayong* curriculum was systematically organized. On January 27, 1971, Air Kuning in Taiping was established as the highest *gayong* training center in Malaysia. In the same year, the new Sultan of Perak, Sultan Idris Shah, awarded Meor Rahman a *Darjah Kebesaran Paduka Cura Si Manja Kini* (Medal of Honor for his merit to the country), entitling him to be called *dato*. A few years later, Sultan Idis Shah joined *gayong* and was given the title *sang sa purba*.

By then, *Dato* Meor's name had become well known throughout Malaysia. His popularity reached the famous Hong Kong martial artist Bruce Lee. While traveling from London to Malaysia with friend Tuan Syed Jamalulail, *Dato* Meor met Bruce Lee at the Hong Kong airport. After introductions, Lee offered him a part in his movie *The Game of Death*. *Dato* Meor respectfully declined the offer. However, they did manage to exchange a few moves, information, and views about Malay and

**Figure 5-6: Meor Rahman in 1975.**

Chinese self-defense. Lee acknowledged the astounding skill of *Dato* Meor Rahman and his *silat seni gayong*.

**Figure 5-7: Bruce Lee.**

*Gayong* continued to broaden, and by 1976 it was estimated that practitioners of *gayong* had reached more than 150,000. Later, the Malaysian army and the Royal Malaysian Police Group started to apply *gayong* as a method of self-defense. Toward the end of 1980, several local and foreign martial artists confronted and challenged *Dato,* but they were all respectfully declined. (Picture on the following page shows *Dato* Meor Rahman in his 70s.)

Toward the end of his life, *Dato* Meor reminded his pupils to always unite. Youngsters were encouraged to learn *gayong* and they were reminded that every *gayong* student is obligated to preserve *silat seni gayong.* On June 23, 1991, *Dato* Meor Abdul Rahman passed away. He was 76 years old. He was buried at Masjid Lama, in Taiping, Perak. His skill in *silat* as a *pendekar* and *mahaguru* is acknowledged by society. Before he died, *Dato* Meor told all *gayong* practitioners that there would be no more *mahaguru* of *silat seni gayong* after his death. *Silat seni gayong* is entrusted to the committees that govern the *gayong* organization. Before he passed away, he selected his daughter, *Cikgu* Siti Kalsom, as the first *gayong* trustee, and *Cikgu* Razali Salleh as the second. *Cikgu* Razali passed away in early 2001.

There are four historical *gayong* places of importance that *Dato* Meor Rahman named before he died. These are places that *gayong* students should visit when they have the opportunity.

- Padang Antah Berantah, in the state of Perak. This is where the government of Gangga Negara was formed.

- Padang Sanai, in the state of Kedah. This is where *Mahaguru Dato* Meor Rahman completed his *silat* education.

- Sudong island in Singapore. This is where *gayong* was introduced to the public.

- Sedili, in the state of Johor. What the grandmaster, before he died, cryptically referred to as the *"end of gayong."*

**Figure 5-8:** *Dato* **Meor in his 70s.**

**Figure 5-9: Meor and his daughter, Siti Kalsom.**

CHAPTER *6*

# Gayong Organization Today

Today due to its size, varying locations, and innovative ideas, *gayong* continues its existence under several names. The prominent groups are Pertubuhan Silat Seni Gayong, Pertubuhan Silat Seni Pusaka Gayong, Pertubuhan Silat Seni Gayong Warisan, and Gayong PASAK Singapore.

## Pertubuhan Silat Seni Gayong Malaysia (PSSGM)

PSSGM is currently the largest *gayong* organization and is presently led by *Cikgu* Siti Kalsom, daughter of *Dato* Meor Rahman. (Figure 6-2 shows Siti Kalsom executing a super combat technique.)

Kalsom has been active in *gayong* since she was a teenager and still is today. She was very close to *Dato*—she started learning *gayong* at the age of fourteen and was taught by *Dato* himself as well as other *gayong* instructors. Her training with *Dato* made her a unique *gayong* student. Because there were only a handful of female stu-

Cikgu Siti Kalsom

Figure 6-1

**Figure 6-2: Cikgu Kalsom executing a super combat technique.**

dents at the time, she was frequently forced to train with men and this made her tougher. According to Kalsom, training with *Dato* was difficult, and she had to go through many tests to make herself physically and spiritually strong. Within the *gayong* community, she was known to be very skillful in *keris* (wavy-bladed dagger) fighting. On February 20, 1970, she performed a demonstration to welcome the Japanese Prince Akihito and his wife Michiko to Malaysia. They were amazed with her demonstration and invited her to Japan for the Osaka Expo in 1970. Due to citizenship issues, she was not able to attend; instead, she sent two other *gayong* instructors in her place. The *silat* demonstration in Japan received a standing ovation and surprised the Emperor of Japan. The demonstration was widely publicized by the media throughout Japan.

Kalsom traveled to many places with her father to assist him in teaching *gayong*. At the age of twenty-one, she was assigned to teach at one of the *gayong* centers in Kampong Pandan, in the city of Kuala Lumpur. One day while training, a gentleman named Mr. Omar introduced himself and challenged her. Mr. Omar was a martial artist from a different discipline. The challenge was accepted and the combat began. Kalsom admitted that Mr. Omar's kicks were powerful, but she ultimately defeated him. Later, they became good friends. Kalsom was chosen to teach *gayong* to 100 selected Malaysian army members from various places within Malaysia.

Before *Dato* Meor died, he told Kalsom, "I will teach you all about

Figure 6-3: Wajadiri training center in Kuala Lumpur, Malaysia.

*gayong* because I want you to take my place when I am gone. I could have been a millionaire if I wanted to and the most respected martial artist in the world, but I choose not to do so. My spirit is for *gayong* and this nation. Guard this *gayong* carefully!"

The pictures below show one of the *gayong* centers, Wajadiri, in Kuala Lumpur, Malaysia.

Figure 6-4: Wajadiri training center.

**Figure 6-5:  Cikgu Majid Mat Isa.**

Gayong Pusaka
Headquarters

**Figure 6-6:  Gayong Pusaka training center in Kedah, Malaysia.**

# Pertubuhan Silat Seni Pusaka Gayong Malaysia (PSSPGM)

PSSPGM is currently led by *Cikgu* Majid Mat Isa. The organization was formed in 1978. *Cikgu* Majid is the chairperson and chief instructor of *pusaka gayong.*

Majid began learning *gayong* in 1957 at the age of eighteen. He studied *gayong* under *Dato* Meor, his father Daeng Uda Mohd Hashim, and his brother Meor Abdul Aziz. He also learned from earlier *gayong* instructors such as *Cikgu* Ismail Mansor and *Cikgu* Kamari Melan from Singapore. As a *gayong* instructor, Majid has taught in several other Malaysian states such as Johor, Melaka, Negeri Sembilan, Pahang, Terengganu, Kelantan, Perak, Selangor, Perlis, Penang, and Medan, Indonesia.

Majid was known to have single-handedly fought forty-five gangsters to protect the village of Pekan Bukit Jenun in the state of Kedah. His act of bravery made him known as *hulubalang legenda* (the legendary Malay warrior). He was given a *Pingat Jasa Kebaktian* Medal of Honor by the Sultan of Kedah.

The headquarters of *pusaka gayong* is presently located in Kampong Kepala Bukit, Gurun, Kedah. Under the teaching of Majid, many outstanding students have emerged as *gayong* instructors.

# Pertubuhan Silat Seni Gayong Warisan Serantau (PSSGWS)

*Cikgu* Mat Nanyang currently leads PSSGWS. This organization was established in 1992, about a year after the death of *Dato* Meor Rahman. The headquarters is in Alor Star, Kedah, in Malaysia and the organization is active mostly in the northern states. The main training center is in Kampong Kepayang, Ipoh, Perak. *Cikgu* Badek Ruzaman is the chief instructor of Gayong Warisan.

# Silat Seni Gayong PASAK Singapura (SSGPS)

*Cikgu* Hussein Kaslan and his son *Cikgu* Mohammad Rahim are leaders of SSGPS. PASAK stands for Perkumpulan Angkatan Sandiwara Anak anak Kesenian (Singapore Youth Society of Dramatic Culture).

Hussein was one of the earliest *gayong* students of *Dato* Meor Rahman in Singapore. Hussein began learning *gayong* in 1950. After 1960, before *Dato* Meor migrated to the state of *Kedah* in Malaysia, he entrusted *gayong* to Hussein to continue its propagation. Hussein is the *imam khalifah* of *gayong* Singapore, with the title of *seri mahkota agung relang pelangi* given by *Dato*. Hussein is *Dato* Meor's right-hand instructor in Singapore. As the *gayong* leader in Singapore, he organized and formed the group PASAK in 1963, known as Gayong PASAK Singapore. The movement of Gayong PASAK under his leadership is successful and is widely accepted by the public. Whenever there

**Figure 6-7: A special patch for Gayong instructors only.**

are national ceremonies, PASAK is always invited to demonstrate. The round logo on figure 6-7 shows a patch that *gayong* instructors wear if they are a *gayong* instructor in the PASAK organization.

Hussein is now over 80 years old. He has endorsed his son Mohammad Rahim to continue the *gayong* mission, culture, and tradition. The picture in figure 6-9 shows *Cikgu* Rahim accepting the leadership role from his father Hussein Kaslan to lead Gayong PASAK in Singapore.

**Figure 6-8:** *Cikgu* **Hussein Kaslan—** *gayong pasak.*

**Figure 6-9: Passing a leadership role to Cikgu Rahim.**

# *Gayong* Internationally

In the United States, *gayong* propagates under the name United States Gayong Federation (USGF), currently led by the author *Cikgu* Sam and *Cikgu* Joel Champ in Chicago, Illinois. There is also a Gayong America group in New Jersey run by Bill Reid under the supervision of *Cikgu* Sulaiman Shariff. Before that, *Cikgu* Shaharudin had introduced *gayong* to a few martial artists in southern Illinois.

*Cikgu* Ariffin Mahidin and *Cikgu* Adlin currently lead *gayong* in the United Kingdom. Some of their students spent four months in Malaysia to continue their *gayong* studies.

*Cikgu* Mufti Ansari was the first person to propagate *gayong* in France in the late 1980s. After he left the country, his students carried on *gayong* activity.

There are students who brought *gayong* to other countries as well, such as Mohammed Moncef Abdullah Al-Querghi in Tunisia and Kuwait and Jan de Jong in western Australia.

In July 2000, *Cikgu* Ridzuan Abdul Razak established *gayong* on the island of Mauritius. Mauritius is located approximately 550 miles

**Figure 6-10: Pictures above from left to right: the author, Ariffin Mahidin, Sulaiman Shariff.**

**Figure 6-10: Pictures above from left to right: Mufti Ansari, Joel Champ, Jan De Jong, and Bill Reid.**

Gayong Malaysia          Gayong UK          United States Gayong Federation

Gayong Pusaka Malaysia          Gayong Warisan Malaysia          Gayong Singapura

Figure 6-11: *Gayong* patches worldwide.

east of Madagascar and about 1,250 miles off the nearest point of the African coast.

## Contributions of Razali Salleh to Gayong

The history of *silat seni gayong* is incomplete without mentioning the great merit and outstanding contributions of *Cikgu* Razali Salleh within the organization. He is considered the brainchild of proliferating and popularizing *silat seni gayong* throughout Malaysia.

**Figure 6-12**

    *Cikgu* Razali started training in *gayong* in 1964. When exposed to *gayong,* Razali saw the potential of the art and took the initiative to involve more people in the group. With his promotion, *gayong* activities became well known within the state of Selangor, where Razali resides. *Gayong* began to spread rapidly, and many invitations were made to demonstrate the art of *gayong. Dato* himself was amazed and attended the demonstration seeking the person responsible for multiplying *gayong* in Selangor. Because of Razali's excellent contributions to *gayong,* the center of *gayong* was eventually relocated from Alor Star in the state of Kedah to Kuala Lumpur, in Selangor. Razali was made the secretary general of *silat seni* Gayong Malaysia.

    Razali did not focus his time completely learning the fighting art. Instead he supported *Dato* Meor Rahman in spreading *gayong* and was involved in administration and organization. Razali became very close to *Dato* and devoted himself to *gayong* goals and objectives.

    Under Razali's administration, *gayong* spread from small provinces to big cities—to high schools, universities, and colleges. He organized many *gayong* groups to venture to states including Perak, Pahang,

**Figure 6-13:  Razali endorsing the author, U.S.**

Terengganu, and Kelantan to establish Gayong grounds. His successful activities made *gayong* known throughout Malaysia. As *gayong*
became more popular, many high-ranking Malaysian government

**Figure 6-14: Razali endorsing *Cikgu* Ariffin Mahidin, U.K.**

officials—including the late prime minister of Malaysia Tun Razak, and Malaysian special army troops began to join. Many national celebrations such as Malaysian Independence Day and Asian Olympic Games began to include *gayong* demonstrations and activities. The reputation of *gayong* grew exponentially and under Razali's leadership, many new skilled instructors emerged. Internationally, Razali had endorsed several of his representatives to spread *gayong* to other countries such as Kuwait, Tunisia, France, Great Britain, and the United States. The following photos show *Cikgu* Razali endorsing his representatives to spread *gayong* to the outside world.

There are others not pictured here such as Sulaiman Shariff for the United States and Mohammad Moncef for Tunisia and Kuwait.

When *Dato* Meor Rahman died in 1991, it was his wish that *Cikgu* Razali be made the second *gayong* trustee with *Dato's* daughter *Cikgu*

Siti Kalsom as the first. Razali was entrusted to keep *Dato's gayong* possessions such as his uniform, medals of honor, personal *keris,* and *bugis sundang* weapons. *Cikgu* Razali and his family were with *Dato* when he passed away.

Under Kalsom and Razali's administration, *gayong* continues to expand. *Cikgu* Razali Salleh died in early 2001 while performing his pilgrimage to Mecca in Saudi Arabia. No other person has taken his place as the second *gayong* trustee. Because *Cikgu* Kalsom is now the only *gayong* trustee recognized by the present *gayong* community, the path of *gayong* at this point lies in the hands of *Cikgu* Siti Kalsom. *Cikgu* Razali's contribution to the success of *gayong* will always be appreciated and recognized.

CHAPTER *7*

# Adat Istiadat Gayong— Gayong Customs

It is customary in *gayong* that before you are accepted as a student, you have to go through an initiation ceremony by completing the *ikrar* (oath) and the *adat mandi tapak* (path shower). This officially welcomes a student of *silat seni gayong*. Anyone wishing to study *gayong* must bring several items for his *mandi tapak,* including a lime, banana, tamarind, and needles. The *gayong* representative will slice the lime as a gesture to accept the student who will then be called *anak gayong* (*gayong* child). The student will bathe with limewater to complete the ceremony. The student is then allowed the privilege to learn the secrets of *gayong*.

There is also a ceremony called *mandi seni* (art or skill bath) for the beginning of weapons training. This ceremony is for students who are ready to enter into the art of weaponry. One must go through this ceremony before training with any weapons. The ceremonial items to bring are almost the same as in *mandi tapak,* with some additional items such as seven differ-

**Figure 7-1:** *Mandi Seni*—**weaponry practice ritual.**

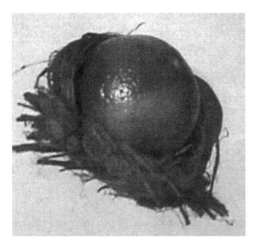

**Figure 7-2: A lime wrapped by a *sintok*.**

ent species of flowers and a candle. At the end of the process, the student will bathe with limewater and flowers to conclude the ceremony. The *mandi tapak* ceremony is only for the male gender and *mandi seni* is for both genders. These are the ceremonies rooted in the philosophy and culture of *gayong,* which are called *adat istiadat* (Malay cultures and traditions), morals, and *adab* (respect).

In general, the *ikrar* (oath) is simply a pledge of loyalty to country, faith, teacher, parents, and *gayong* members. The items brought in for the ceremony are symbolic. You will taste a pinch of salt and tamarind, which symbolizes the bitter and sweet moments of life and *gayong* training. The needles are symbols of how sharp and treacherous *gayong* can be—they will be thrown into the sea at a later time. The lime is regarded as a fruit that cures many diseases; taking a bath with limewater indicates cleansing of the body. The *sintok,* similar to coconut husks, is used as a sponge to rub the body. The banana is for the *gayong* group to eat to signify the benefits of training and the knowledge as a reward—a fruitful result. As for the flowers, they signify nature, and the fragrance and beauty of the art—the *seni.* The candle is a symbol of a light that shines in order for others to see the way.

CHAPTER *8*

# Gayong Philosophy

The best defense is simply to not be in the position of having to defend oneself. This is true in all self-defense systems, and *gayong* is no exception. In *gayong,* religion is the inspiration, motivation, and guidance for high-quality behavior. Religion teaches one to be kindhearted, patient, and moderate in all things, and compassionate to all. An old saying in *gayong* is, *"Kata bersahut gayong bersambut,"* which means, "Diplomacy must be adopted before hostility." The meaning of *kata bersahut* is dialogue or negotiations, and *gayong bersambut* comes afterward, which indicates that *gayong* should absolutely be the last alternative.

Figure 8-1: A symbol of balance.

A *silat* practitioner must never misuse his art, as that would be in direct violation of trust with the Creator, He who is truly the "Most Gracious, Most Merciful." It is He who has given practitioners the skills and knowledge of *silat*. These qualities and beliefs are found in the prayer that is recited at the beginning of *silat* training classes. The prayer begins, "In The Name of GOD, Most Gracious, Most Merciful." True strength comes from unity of body, mind, heart, and with the Almighty. A true *silat* practitioner is never one to inflame confrontations, but rather steer clear of them through positive thoughts and

**Figure 8-2: Quran—the holy book of Islam.**

actions. "... begin not hostilities. GOD loves not aggressors ... GOD is Forgiving, Merciful ... then let there be no hostility." (2:190-193) (The number two indicates *surah* or chapter two of the Quran, and the number 190-193 indicates verses 190 through 193.)

But beware! When conditions have called upon the *silat* practitioner to really defend himself, nothing can stop the *silat* practitioner unless the opponent ceases first. As prescribed, "Permission [to fight] is granted to those who are being persecuted, since injustice has fallen them, and GOD is well able to assist."(22:39) (This verse was revealed when the followers of Islam were murdered and oppressed by their enemies merely because they were following their faith. Therefore, they were predestined to stand up and protect themselves, and the major battle of Badr took place in 2 Hijra, 624 A.D.)

War is not an objective nor is it the normal course of action. It is only the last resort and is used under the most extraordinary circumstances. "Fighting is prescribed for you, and you dislike it. But it is possible that you dislike a thing which is good for you, and that you love a thing, which is bad for you. GOD knows, and you know not." (2:216).

A true *silat* practitioner does not simply learn a method of self-defense. It is also a philosophical, healing, spiritual, and cultural study. *Belajar mengenal diri* (learning to know oneself) is learning to be a kind, humble, pleasant, and favorable human being. As the late *Mahaguru Dato* Meor Abdul Rahman used to say, *"Sehati, sejiwa, sekendi, sejalan, sedarah, sedaging, sepadu."* (One heart, one soul, one form, one destiny, one blood, one flesh, one entity.)

# CHAPTER 9

# The Meaning of Gayong

*Gayong* in *Jawi* letters (Arabic alphabet) is spelled *Ga, Alif, Ya, Wau, Nga.*

> **Ga—Genggam.** Uphold the teachings of one's faith; strong determination to achieve and understand the philosophy and secrets of *gayong* and to hold in trust the master's teachings.
>
> **Alif—Angkat.** Uphold the teachings of one's faith as the guidance of life.
>
> **Ya—Yakin.** Confidence—one must be brave for the sake of truth.
>
> **Wau—Waras.** Common sense and rationality—one must weigh all consequences vigilantly before taking action.
>
> **Nga—Ngeri.** One's fear of the Almighty.

The *gayong* symbol was originally inspired by *Dato* Meor and designed by a great scholar, Zaba. The original *gayong* symbol had only one dragon. The second

**Figure 9-1:** *Gayong* in *Jawi* writing.

**Figure 9-2:** Old *gayong* logo—two dragons.

**Figure 9-3:** Current *gayong* logo—one dragon.

dragon was later added in appreciation to *Dato* Meor's elder brother, Meor Abdul Aziz. Later, the original symbol returned and has been used since.

*Bulan dan bintang* (**moon and star**)—symbolize faith as the guiding force of our existence.

*Bumi* (**world**)—represents that the art will be introduced and propagated to all nations.

*Naga dan harimau* (**dragon and tiger**)—represent strength in water and on land.

*Keris dan parang* (**dagger and machete**)—represent Malay traditional weapons and culture.

**The sword of** *zulfakar* (**Arabian blade**)—reminds us of the warriors that defended the teaching of faith and truth in the era of the uncivilized world.

*Keris bersilang* (**two crossed daggers**)—represent the spirit of the two legendary Malay warriors, Hang Tuah and Hang Jebat. This *keris* is the well-known *keris* called Taming Sari.

*Bengkong hitam* (*mahaguru* **personal black belt**)—The Malay *bengkung* or *selempang* represents *adat* (tradition). The name of the belt is *Harimau Pelangi Cula Sakti Gangga Negara*. It is the highest belt in *silat seni gayong*. *Bengkung* signifies a custom rich with tradition, culture, and respect. Dato Meor's personal belt is called *Bengkung Harimau Pelangi Agong Mahkota Sakti*.

**The connotation of color in:**

*Putih* (white)—Purity and Honesty

*Merah* (red)—Bravery

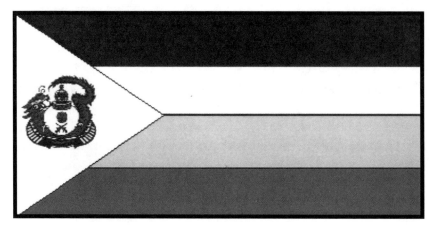

**Figure 9-4: The flag of *silat seni gayong* Malaysia.**

*Kuning* (yellow)—Royalty

*Hitam* (black)—Equality. Black is the color of shadow. It symbolizes social status. Our shadow makes no distinction among us in
regards to race, gender, or status, thus symbolizing equality. The
shadow also means that we are our own worst enemy.

# CHAPTER 10

# Gayong Forms

*Silat* generally consists of two forms, the soft form and the hard form. The soft form is referred to as *bunga* (flowery dance), or *kembangan*. The soft form in *gayong* can also be called *tapak sembah* (presentation steps). The hard form is referred to as *tapak hulubalang* (warrior steps). *Gayong* uses both soft and hard forms. Soft form is practiced only on certain occasions, such as in demonstrations or salutations in front of the king and queen. In general, *bunga* movements have fighting moves, which are linked together in dance. The dance has a story behind the actions; the story relates to nature, culture, tradition, and the Creator. For the most part, *gayong* moves today are hard form—*tapak hulubalang*.

*Gayong* style uses striking, grappling, and bone-breaking techniques. *Buah kunci mati* or *tangkapan* (dead locks or grappling) is typically used to discontinue the opponent's attack. This is the concept of economy of motion. Why waste energy if you can catch and lock your opponent quickly? *Gayong* form uses all parts of the human anatomy. Variations of tangkapan are applied when your opponent is larger or

**Figure 10-1: Super combat technique.**

**Figure 10-2: Super combat technique.**

**Figure 10-3:** *Patah dayong* **technique.**

stronger than you. *Tepis menepis* or *elak men-gelak* (avoidance and blocking) are used if you intend not to engage in a brawl or injure the opponent. Within *tepis menepis,* a strike to a crucial body point can be applied if absolutely unavoidable.

Another category of engagement is *serangan harimau* or tiger attack, sometimes referred to as *serangan maut* (super combat). This is a combination of blows, claws, tears, and pokes to vital points. These movements are applied when offending or attacking while defending. With the exception of *yoi* and *belian, gayong* movements are typically vigorous and explosive, like a tiger ready to devour its prey, when facing a challenger.

*Gayong* teaches the concept of *berimau rimau berimba rimba bergayong*—a survival technique that uses any elements in the surrounding vicinity to avert an oncoming attack. *Gayong* also teaches the ground fighting form. Falling to the ground does not indicate that combat is over and done with. Falling to the ground transforms into employing *gerakan harimau* (tiger movement). Further action would be to control the opponent's center axis by pushing, twisting, joint locking, and off balancing maneuvers.

When you are learning *silat* you will be taught form and body movement. But application, adapting, and adjusting to the opponent's movements is totally up to the individual's instincts.

Even though the techniques used in *gayong* can be depicted as brutal and lethal, the practitioners are reminded constantly to pray to the Creator—never quickly apply the knowledge unless absolutely necessary.

In weapons training, real weapons are normally used. This is to exercise and build the practitioner's confidence when facing an opponent with real weapons. The weapons training

**Figure 10-4:** *Seni siku* **technique.**

includes and not limited to *pisau* (knife), *keris* (dagger), machete, long and short staff, *tekpi* (sai), *lembing* (spear), and others.

As a practitioner matures, the drills are no longer physical, but rather more mental, spiritual, and metaphysical. The practitioner begins to stay away from the rigors of physical movements and devotes most of his time to worship of the Creator.

**Figure 10-5:** *Keris* **technique.**

**Figure 10-6: Jumping over fire.**

**Figure 10-7: Breaking tiles.**

**Figure 10-8: Jumping over multiple people.**

CHAPTER 11

# Gayong Curriculum

It was *Dato's* inspiration that *gayong* curriculum must be updated to keep pace with the needs of the modern combat. Together with his highest-ranking instructors such as *Cikgu* Majid Mat Isa (figure 11-1) and *Cikgu* Awang Daud (figure 11-2) they formulated today's *gayong* curriculum. There are 349 known striking techniques as the core replica that form the empty hand portion of the *gayong* curriculum. Today *gayong* curriculum is fundamentally broken down into seven levels:

1. ***Tapak Gayong***
   Foundation movements: basic punches, blocks, kicks, counters, and recounters

2. ***Seni Tapak Gayong***
   Combative movements: joint-locks, takedowns, and body locks

Figure 11-1            Figure 11-2

3. **Seni Keris**

*Keris,* knife, ex, *kerambit, tekpi* (sai), and *sundang lipas*

4. **Seni Simbat**

Short and long sticks, machetes, and spears

5. **Seni Yoi**

The art of deception

6. **Seni Belian**

The art of tearing and internal strength

7. **Seni Cindai**

The art of *sarong:* rope, veil, chain, and belt

*Gayong* ranking system is divided into six categories:

1. *Bengkung hitam*—Beginner black belt

2. *Pelangi puteh*—White rainbow or white belt

3. *Pelangi hijau*—Green rainbow or green belt

4. *Pelangi merah*—Red rainbow or red belt (three stripes)

5. *Pelangi kuning*—Yellow rainbow or yellow belt (five stripes)

6. *Pelangi hitam harimau cula sakti*—Black rainbow mystical tiger stripes (black belt up to six stripes only—the seventh stripe is only for the Grand Master *Dato* Meor Abdul Rahman)

The *bengkung* (belt) system was not implemented until 1970. The old belt system simply used a cloth about four to five inches wide wrapped around the waist twice.

**Figure 11-3:** *Pelangi hitam gayong* **black belt.**

# CHAPTER 12

# Kebatinan (Spirituality)

In *silat, kebatinan* is internal and in the heart, hidden, and mysterious. This is the most difficult stage to achieve in learning *silat. Kebatinan* means one who searches to develop inner tranquility and the *rasa diri* (an intuitive inner feeling) through a method of self-submission. One may experience intuitively the divine presence of the Almighty residing within the heart. This is the awakening of the heart and a special knowledge like an unseen treasure that only those who recognize the essence of the Almighty can discover. The practitioner of *kebatinan*

**Figure 12-1: The mountain of Hira
in Saudi Arabia.**

seeks to cultivate the true self, achieving harmony, and ultimately unity. Achieving *kebatinan* is quite strenuous; it is a search to develop good and noble character. It is a personal search of an intuitive connection to the Almighty, and a positive way of life.

*Kebatinan* may be practiced in Islam, Hinduism, Buddhism, Christianity, or any other religious or mystical movement. *Kebatinan* for Muslims is steeped in the Islamic faith. Anything beyond that is considered as *shirk* (associating partners with Allah).

**Figure 12-2: Quran—the holy book of Islam.**

# CHAPTER 13

# Distinction of the Keris in Silat

The *keris* (sometimes spelled *kris*) is a distinctive, double-edged, wavy-bladed dagger with blade lengths ranging from five to thirty inches long. The *keris* varies to a large extent in shape and size depending on local flavor. The primary use of the *keris* is for thrusting. The *keris* is the principle weapon used throughout Malaysia and Indonesia and is regarded as the national weapon. It is also widely used by *silat* practitioners in the Philippine islands. The origin of the *keris* is rather uncertain. Some say that the weapons have Indonesian characteristics with the influence of Indian weapons, which were transferred to the Malay Peninsula.

The *keris* is a hallmark of social and cultural distinction. It has become a royal sovereign symbol, particularly as ceremonial dress. For instance, a unique *keris* is used in the ceremony of establishing a new king of Malaysia every five years. (Figure 13-2 shows the XII King of Malaysia, Tuanku Syed Sirajuddin Ibni Al-Marhum

**Figure 13-1: The Malay *keris*.**

**Figure 13-2: The XII Malaysian king.**

**Figure 13-3:** *Keris* **is part of the culture in a wedding ceremony.**

Tuanku Syed Putra Jamallail.) In the marriage ceremony, the *keris* is worn by the groom and signifies a status of *raja dan permaisuri sehari* (king and queen for a day—see figure 13-3). Most *silat* grand masters usually own a distinctive *keris* with a special design. Within *silat,* any special ceremony will always include the *keris.* It is customary that when learning *silat,* you will also learn how to handle the *keris* properly. In any *silat* you learn, the *keris* will always be a part of the syllabus. There is an old saying, "A *silat* without a knife or *keris* is not *silat.*"

There are many superstitions and fables associated with the *keris.* For instance, many people have heard that the *keris* will rattle in its sheath to warn the owner that danger is approaching. The *keris* is said to have the power of *tuju tuju* (similar to sorcery), which is highly feared by Malay society. Whatever it is, this power can be either beneficial or wicked. In the fifteenth century, the legendary Malay warrior Hang Tuah was known to be the owner of the distinguished *keris* called Taming Sari. It was said that anyone who possessed this *keris* would have the power of invincibility. It was this lethal *keris* that killed Hang Tuah's childhood friend, Hang Jebat, who was disloyal to the sultan of Malacca. Every *keris* has a story; they are tales of adventure, nobility, tradition, and romance.

Traditionally, a real *keris* is used during practice. You must focus sharply on what you are doing. Any small error may cause a great deal of harm. The first stage of learning the *keris* in *gayong* is to learn all of the *jurus* (basic movements). Next, you will learn the *keris pentas* (preset counter and recounter movements). From *pentas* extend all sorts of technique variations that are considered *buah keris*. They are varieties similar to the variation of *buah kunci mati* (body lock techniques).

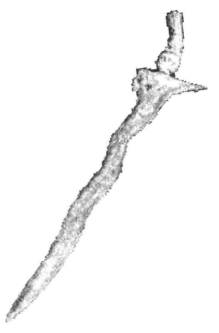

**Figure 13-4:  Taming Sari**

In *gayong,* the culmination of learning *keris* takes place by the seaside. At the end of the ceremony all students join hands and walk into the ocean (about four feet deep), led by a woman, and submerge into the seawater. (In *gayong,* woman is the

**Figure 13-5:  End of *keris* training ritual.**

**Figure 13-6:  *Keris* training before the ritual.**

**Figure 13-7:** *Keris* **monument in Port Kelang, Malaysia.**

mother, the head of the dragon.) The plunge is done for a duration of three seconds. This is done three times. When this is finished, *keris* practice in *gayong* is *tamat* (complete) and it is now up to the individual to perfect their techniques. (Figure 13-7 shows a *keris* monument near Port Kelang, Selangor, Malaysia.)

Further readings about *keris* can be found in a book titled *The Kris: Mystic Weapon of the Malay World*, by Edward Frey. Another book is *Origin of the Keris and Its Development to the 14th Century*, by A.G. Maisey.

CHAPTER 14

# Message to All Practitioners

It is rational to say that all systems of martial art have strong and weak points; each is unique and stands on its own. The essential point is that there is no superior art. It is an art! Therefore, it is a learning process. The essence of learning self-defense is sincerity, loyalty, righteousness, humility, and the ability to change and to sincerely accept each of these as elements of integration. Pride, ego, greed, arrogance, miserliness, and jealousy are qualities that will gradually destroy.

Remember, Satan was once among the angels, but because of his pride, ego, and feeling of superiority he become the Devil!

"There is a piece of organ in human's body—when it is in a good state, the whole being improves, and when it is in a bad state, the whole being falls apart. Beware, that piece of organ is the heart."*

**Figure 14-1**

---

*The collected sayings and biography of Prophet Muhammad (peace be upon him), forming the second great religious text of Islam after the Quran. The Quran is the Holy Book of Islam.

---

CHAPTER *15*

# Gayong Techniques

*Gayong* curriculum is commonly divided into seven different categories. Each category concentrates on specific skills and principles. In the early days, each category possessed somewhat limited techniques and the teaching procedures were very unstructured. Consequently, these techniques were formulated, revised, analyzed, and reorganized by the late *Mahaguru* Meor Rahman and his high-ranking instructors to keep pace with modern combat needs. In early *silat,* each category contained only seven techniques. Later, *pecahan* (variations) were added to each movement and the techniques became limitless. For that reason, twenty-one basic replica techniques were chosen for each category as a standard. After mastering the twenty-one replica techniques, it is up to the individual to implement the *pecahan* for each technique. Each technique variation subsequently becomes infinite. Each technique should be treated as alive and should adapt intelligently and skillfully depending on circumstances.

In every technique there are always one or more counter techniques. Within each category, a routine called *pentas* (counter and re-counter attacks) was formed. The original name for *pentas* was *seni gulung* (tangle or intertwine and un-tangle). *Pentas* exists within empty-hand techniques as well as weapon techniques. The intention of *pentas* is to train the body to establish a behavior that rationally reacts

and defends automatically when being attacked. This is a habit that one must continuously practice to get accustomed to the behavior.

It is impossible to cover all of the techniques within a single book. This book has illustrations for just some of the categories. Perhaps, in the near future, another book will include other categories.

It is customary that before the training begins, a *gayong silat* practitioner will remember the Almighty and pray for the safety of all members.

The figure above shows *gayong* practitioners sitting down for the *buka gelanggang* (open training ritual) before beginning *gayong* training. Generally, the ritual is done as a group. All practitioners are required to clear their minds, to pray or to meditate for the safety of all members, and for the knowledge learned to benefit all. Following the ritual, the norm is to warm-up before beginning to learn *silat* techniques. The exercises are for loosening up all joints and muscles.

The figure at left shows a basic stance. The person on the right (the attacker) is on his horse stance position and is ready to deliver a forward step punch. The defender generally stands with two legs open about shoulder width apart in a horse stance perpendicular to the opponent's.

# ☀ Basic Rolling

**Figure 15-1-1**

1                    2                    3

4                    5

Unlike other martial arts which practice diagonal rolls starting from one side of your shoulder and ending up on the opposite side of your hip, *gayong* practices rolling similar to gymnastic rolling. Rolling in *silat* is used in many different ways, such as to minimize pain when falling, jumping from one position to the next, jumping over an obstacle or through narrow openings, making a distance jump to grab a weapon, or falling while holding a dangerous weapon. The image above shows a *silat* practitioner performing a forward roll. It is critical that you tuck in your head before rolling forward on the ground. Your legs should be open about shoulder width apart when you are ready to get up again.

## ☀ Principles of Defensive Body Movements

The concept of body angle movements when defending yourself is to step away from the attacker's line of force and terminate the aggressor's motion by repositioning yourself at the aggressor's weakest angle and executing the tech- nique. Although in the old days the majority of *silat* practitioners were never made aware of the scientific basis behind movement maneuvering; the theory of circle and points were unconsciously taught by practical angle manipulation. The concept can be visualized by a circle with a centerline as a reference and cut into twelve different slices or angles (see figure 15-2-1).

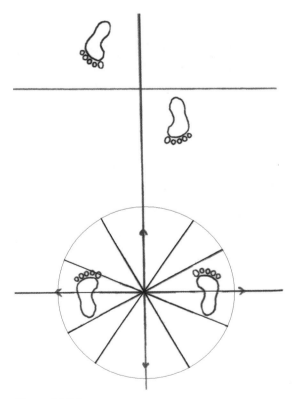

**Figure 15-2-1**

The circle represents the area of your security. You are not in danger as long as your opponent does not enter the circular area. Generally, the length of your leg can calculate the diameter of your circle security area. Just extend your leg straight at a ninety-degree angle and spin around. That will be your imaginary circle area. When your opponent enters the circle or attacks you, you have the option to move at any of the angles shown, depending on your opponent's line of force or entrance point. This is a concept also used by other martial arts styles.

## ☀ *Silat* **Basic Block**

Basic blocks in *silat* are very critical. They are the foundation upon which to build other movements in the follow-up techniques. Each basic block can be broken down into many different ways. The movements are limitless once the understanding of the basic block strategy is truly mastered.

Before the basic block is taught, a *silat* practitioner must learn the *asas gerakkan* and *gulungan*. These are the very basic self-defense movements that everyone needs to know. These movements are sometimes referred to as *jurus*.

*Seni gayong silat* teaches seven different sets of blocks. Each block is broken into seven different techniques. Each technique can yet be broken into several more techniques. For the purpose of understanding the basic block foundation, two sets will be illustrated in this book—*asas elakkan one* and *asas elakkan two* (basic block set one and basic block set two). *Asas elakkan* can sometimes be referred to as *tepis menepis,* which simply means avoidance techniques.

## *Asas Elakkan Satu* (Basic Block Set One, One through Seven)

**Figure 15-3-1:** *Tangkis luar* (outside block).

1                                                              2

The above figures show that when a punch is delivered you can use an outside block. Move your body back by whirling your right foot back in a clockwise direction and stopping at an angle of about 135 degrees, stepping away from your opponent's line of force and blocking their right arm punch with your left forearm from outside in. You also have the alternative to turn 180 degrees and then block. Notice that your right arm is in a ready position to follow-up the next move, if necessary. All blocks can be practiced on both sides.

**Figure 15-3-2:** *Tangkis atas* (**upward block**).

1                                                    2

In this upper block, when the opponent delivers the punch, move your left foot forward at a forty-five-degree angle with your left forearm blocking your opponent's punch upward, redirecting your opponent's line of force slightly to their right side. Note that your body is slightly perpendicular to their body, giving you more force and energy to execute any follow-up moves, if necessary. When blocking with your left forearm, you have the option to make a fist or an open palm. With either option, you may continue the technique by stretching out your left arm and using the palm to strike your opponent's face immediately after the block execution.

**Figure 15-3-3:** *Tangkis bawah* (**downward block**).

1                                              2

In this lower block, move your right foot back at a forty-five-degree angle with your left upper forearm blocking your opponent's punch downward, redirecting their line of force slightly to their right side. Your right arm is ready to execute the next move if needed.

**Figure 15-3-4:** *Elak luar mara, tangkis, balas tumbuk*
(**Forward outside block with punch to floating ribs**).

1                                              2

To execute a forward outside block with a punch to their floating ribs, move your body to your left side at a forty-five-degree angle, stepping forward with your right foot going in a straight line slightly to the right of your opponent, and simultaneously block your opponent's punch with your left hand at their elbow by pushing their arm out and at the same time delivering your punch straight to their floating ribs. Your block is done with an open palm. The block can either be a push or a tap to your right side.

**Figure 15-3-5:** *Elak kilas tangan kebawah balas tending ke dada* (**Twisting hand block followed by a roundhouse to chest**).

1          2          3

To execute a hand twist and a kick to their chest, move your right foot back in a clockwise direction at a ninety-degree angle and simultaneously catch your opponent's right wrist with both hands and twist in a down and upward motion making a semicircle movement toward your left side. This creates momentum in your right leg and the ability to deliver a powerful roundhouse kick to their abdomen or chest.

**Figure 15-3-6:** *Elak dalam balas rodok ulu hati* (**Inside block followed by thrusting to solar plexus**).

1

2

To execute a right hand thrust to their solar plexus, move your right foot forward toward your opponent's body by stepping inside at a forty-five-degree angle while blocking their punch with your left forearm with an open palm, and simultaneously delivering a straight thrust punch to your opponent's solar plexus.

**Figure 15-3-7:** *Elak pijak pelipat kaki dan serangan pancung tengkok* (**Blocking by stepping on back of opponent's knee followed up by striking the back of their neck**).

1

2

3

To execute a strike to the back of their neck, step forward with your right foot at an angle of forty-five degrees while your right hand grabs the opponent's right upper arm for balance maneuvering. Simultaneously pin down the back of your opponent's right knee with your right foot, which brings them down. Then strike the back of their neck with your right hand; this technique can be followed up with multiple strikes if necessary.

## Asas Elakkan Dua (Basic Block Set Two, One through Seven)

This category of block applies kicking techniques. The target areas are the: floating ribs, the armpit, the shoulder joint, the forearm, and the elbow (good for disarming weapons or changing the opponent's direction of force), the solar plexus, the calf, and the neck. There are other body areas that can be the target, but are not shown in this book, such as the knee, the thigh, the groin, and the abdomen.

**Figure 15-3-8:** *Sepak juring kanan ke rusuk kanan* (**Sidekick to right floating ribs or upper ribs**).

1            2            3

Figure 15-3-8 shows a kick to their right ribs. When the opponent delivers a punch, move your body a little to your left, stepping out slightly away from your opponent's straight line of force. Deliver your right sidekick straight to your opponent's armpit or upper ribs while your right hand holds their right wrist.

**Figure 15-3-9:** *Sepak juring kiri ke rusuk kanan*
(**Sidekick to left floating ribs**).

1                    2                    3

The above technique is the same as the one shown in figure 15-3-8, except that it is done on the opposite side. Move your body a little to your right, stepping slightly away from your opponent's straight line of force. Deliver your left sidekick straight to your opponent's armpit or upper ribs while your left hand holds their right wrist.

**Figure 15-3-10:** *Libasan kaki kanan ke lengan penyerang*
(**Right leg roundhouse step-push to opponent's arm**).

1                    2                    3

In figure 15-3-10, your aim is to block and redirect the opponent's punch or line of force away from you. Move your body slightly to your right, away from your opponent's straight line of force, simultaneously swinging your right leg outside in, aiming at your opponent's forearm. It is important to strike the area between your opponent's wrist and elbow section. This gives you a greater control to change your opponent's body position and the direction of their force.

**Figure 15-3-11:** *Libasan kaki kiri ke lengan penyerang*
**(Left leg roundhouse step-push to opponent's elbow).**

1                            2                            3

Figure 15-3-11 is similar to figure 15-3-10, except it is on the opposite side. Move your body slightly to your left, away from your opponent's line of force, simultaneously swinging your left leg outside in, aiming at your opponent's elbow. It is important to strike the elbow to get greater control in order to change your opponent's body position and direction of force.

**Figure 15-3-12:** *Sepak layang kanan ke dada* (**Right roundhouse to opponent's chest**).

1                              2                              3

When the punch is delivered, move your body to your left, away from your opponent's line of force, while catching your opponent's punch by their wrist for balance maneuvering. Simultaneously pivot your body to the left side and deliver a roundhouse kick with your right leg to their chest or abdomen. All kicking techniques shown above can be followed up by more striking if necessary.

**Figure 15-3-13:** *Sepak layang kanan ke belakang penyerang* (**Front side kick using side foot to back of opponent**).

1                              2                              3

This technique is similar to the one in figure 15-3-12, except that the kick is now targeted at the back of your opponent's body. Move your body to your right, stepping away from the opponent's line of force while catching the opponent's punch by their wrist for balance maneuvering. Simultaneously delivering the reverse kick. The target area can be your opponent's lower back or their kidney.

**Figure 15-3-14:** *Sauk kaki kanan dengan kaki kiri balas juring ke leher* (**Sweep the right leg of your opponent with left leg followed by a sidekick to the neck**).

1      2      3

4      5

When the opponent delivers their punch, make a small hop to your left, stepping away from the opponent's line of force and positioning yourself at a ninety-degree angle, perpendicular to your opponent's force line. Simultaneously grab with your right hand your opponent's wrist, and hold your opponent's shoulder with your left hand for balance maneuvering. Position your left leg back, making yourself ready to execute a sweep to the back of your opponent's right leg. The sweep is executed with your left leg while your left hand simultaneously pulls your opponent's shoulder back with a downward motion. Hold on to their right hand and quickly change hands when your opponent is on the ground. Finally, execute a straight down motion kick to their throat, chin, or face.

## ☀ Buah Tapak and Pecahan (Body Lock Techniques and Variations)

The concept of *buah tapak* is to grab hold of and lock the opponent's body to end the aggressor's violent behavior. The *buah tapak* technique uses all parts of the anatomy, and the end result of *buah tapak* is devastating. When executing the technique, the defender has the option to complete the technique or to deviate the technique to other movements. While catching the opponent, takedowns and joint-locks are applied. Most lock movements apply bone-breaking techniques by putting pressure to joints and tendons, reversing the joint's anatomy and muscles by twisting, pushing, or pulling. *Buah tapak* is sometimes also referred to as *tangkapan* (catching) or simply *buah* (fruit).

Each lock movement is given a metaphorical name. The entrance of the lock movement may be the same, and may come from different angles or sides, but the finishing of the movement may differ. The variation of the lock depends on the opponent's movement, height, speed, weight, and strength. There are twenty-one basic replicas of body-lock techniques. Each technique can be broken down to many different variations. The following figures show examples of those techniques and some of their variations. The techniques shown are not in any particular order.

**Figure 15-4-1:** *Ular sawa berendam* (sinking python).

1. The opponent delivers their punch.

2. Move your body back by whirling your right foot back in a clockwise direction and stopping at an angle of about 135 degrees, stepping away from your opponent's line of force. Simultaneously catch and hold your opponent's right wrist and block your opponent's right arm with your left forearm from outside in. It is important to block at your opponent's elbow to put pressure and pain on their elbow joint. By doing so, you redirect their force line sideways, making them lean forward.

3. Before your opponent falls forward, reverse the force by folding your opponent's hand slightly toward their right side towards the back of their right shoulder.

4. As your right forearm comes closer to their face, elbow their face with your right elbow and apply pressure by twisting their wrist with your right hand to your left in a downward motion. Your opponent may feel like falling on their back and resisting the force.

5. To equalize your opponent's force, raise your right leg and knee straight to their right floating ribs.

6. Sweep their right leg with your right leg to make them fall to the ground on their back, and maintain the wristlock.

7. Kick straight to their face with your right foot.

8. Transfer your hand lock to your right leg and fold your leg tightly to lock the arm and elbow your opponent's face with your right elbow.

9. Rotate your body slightly to your left and catch your opponent's left leg. Swing it in a sideways upward motion with your two hands (left hand on their knee pushing down and right hand on

their foot pulling up), and lock their leg with your left leg, folding your leg tightly. Notice that you lock your leg with your feet crossing each other. This secures the lock.

10. At this point you have your opponent's body tightly locked and your two arms are free to do anything. Lean your body back a little bit to tighten up the body lock, raise your arms simultaneously, then use your right elbow to hit your opponent's face and your left elbow to hit their groin or abdomen.

11. If your opponent attempts (or is able) to kick your head with their left leg, catch their leg with your right hand and press their leg down toward their face, locking their leg underneath your armpit or straight down underneath your right knee. At this point your opponent is completely deadlocked. Stretching your back further will put more pain on your opponent's body.

**Figure 15-4-2:** *Pecahan ular sawa berendam* (**sinking python variation one**).

1                    2                    3

1. Execute the outside block technique. It is important that you block at your opponent's elbow and simultaneously hold the opponent's right wrist.

2. As soon as your left forearm makes contact with your opponent's

elbow, move your left leg forward and at the same time push your opponent's right elbow in a forward-down motion, forcing their body to go down.

3.  Before your opponent falls to the ground, make a low horse stance with open legs shoulder-width apart. Pull your opponent's right hand across your abdomen, slightly below your navel, with your opponent's elbow pointing upward. Lock their arm with your upper body by leaning slightly forward. Grab and lock your opponent's left arm with your left arm by doing the chicken-wing lock behind their left shoulder, and pull your opponent's head closer to you with your two hands. Positioning your opponent's arm on their back and pulling the hand up towards the back of their neck does a chicken-wing lock. Note that if you make your horse stance lower, you will break your opponent's right elbow.

**Figure 15-4-3:** *Pecahan ular sawa berendam*
**(sinking python variation two).**

1.  When the opponent delivers their punch, move your body back by whirling your right foot back in a clockwise direction and stopping at an angle of about 135 degrees. Step away from your opponent's line of force, while catching and holding your opponent's right wrist and blocking your opponent's punch with your left forearm from outside in. Block at your opponent's elbow to put pressure and pain on their elbow joint. By doing so, you redirect your opponent's force sideways, making them lean forward.

2.  Before the opponent falls forward, reverse the force by folding their arm slightly toward their right side near the right side of their face.

1                        2                        3

4                        5

3.  To weaken your opponent's body, raise your right leg and knee straight to their ribs on the right side of their body.

4.  Pull your opponent's arm over their head and insert their head at the center of your locked arms. Choke your opponent's head with your locked arms and pull them closer to you toward your left side, tightening up the choke. This gives you control of their head, neck, and body.

5.  Position yourself with your left knee on the floor and pull your opponent's body down by placing their lower back on your right knee. At this point your opponent is completely under your control. You may complete your technique by choking your opponent further or pushing their upper body lower to the ground.

**Figure 15-4-4:** *Sangga maut* (**deadly support**).

1. When the opponent delivers their punch, move your right leg back by positioning yourself at about 135 degrees, and simultaneously block their punch with your left forearm from the outside in.

2. Lean forward and swing your right arm, bending your opponent's right elbow from the inside out, and use your left arm to push their right forearm in a down-and-up motion, assisting your right arm in executing the chicken-wing lock on your opponent's right arm.

3. Bend their arm behind their right shoulder, and execute the chicken-wing lock by placing your right arm inside their right arm, behind their right shoulder.

4. Extend your left arm in front of your opponent's face from behind, and wrap your arm tightly around their neck, joining your left hand with your right hand. This will lock your opponent's neck. If you tighten up the neck lock and apply pressure on the left and right sides of their neck by squeezing it firmly, you will cut the oxygen supply to their brain. If you hold the lock for three seconds or more, your opponent will become unconsciousness or even die. Great care must be taken to avoid irreparable harm.

5. Bring your opponent downward by using your left leg to pin down their right knee from behind. Pull your opponent's body back by placing your left knee at their tailbone and pushing forward slightly with your left knee, finally pulling your arms up and back. This motion will utterly break your opponent's backbone and their right shoulder. Great care must be taken to avoid irreparable harm.

1

2

3

4

5

**Figure 15-4-5:** *Cekak banting* (choking throw).

1

2

3

4

5

1. Move your body back by whirling your right foot back in a clockwise direction and stopping at an angle of about 135 degrees. Stepping away from your opponent's line of force and simultaneously raise both of your arms in preparation to strike your opponent's right arm.

2. Strike your opponent's forearm downward.

3. Lean slightly forward and lock your opponent's neck with both of your forearms.

4. Join your hands together and drag their neck to your left shoulder.

5. Drop on your right knee and pull your opponent's upper body downward. Care should be taken not to pull too hard for it may

break your opponent's neck. Great care must be taken to avoid irreparable harm.

**Figure 15-4-6:** *Kacip selak emas* (**golden locked slicer**).

1

2

3

4

5

1. When a punch is delivered, move your right foot back in a clockwise direction at a ninety-degree angle and simultaneously catch your opponent's right wrist with your right hand and position your left arm in preparation to strike their right ribs.

2. Elbow their right ribs with your left elbow. Notice that when you elbow their ribs, your left leg goes behind their right leg.

3. Swing their right arm behind them and simultaneously grab their neck with your left arm and pull yourself closer to them on their right side closing the gap between you and your opponent.

4. Lock your opponent's neck with both of your arms.

5.  Slowly drop your left knee on the back of their right knee and simultaneously pull down their upper body, attempting to join their head to their right knee, sideways. By doing this, you put pain and pressure on the backbone of their right side.

**Figure 15-4-7:** *Tali gantong* (**hanging rope**).

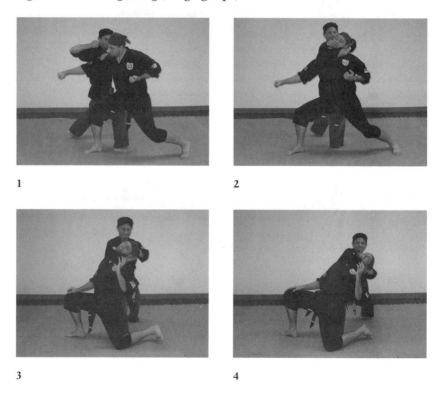

1                               2

3                               4

1.  When a punch is delivered, step out with your right leg to your left side at a forty-five-degree angle and step forward, simultaneously pushing your opponent's elbow with your left hand to your right with an open hand palm. At the same time punch the right side of their face with your right hand fist or palm.

2.  Choke their neck from behind with your right arm and place your

left arm behind their neck, grabbing your left bicep with your right hand. Put your left hand on your opponent's right temple and push to their left side.

3. While choking their neck, pin down their back left knee by stepping on the knee with your right leg.

4. Step back with your left leg behind you and push your opponent's body slightly forward with your right knee. While locking their neck, twist their body to your left side. The lower you go, the more pain is put onto your opponent's neck, head, and lower back.

**Figure 15-4-8:** *Selak mati* (**dead locked**).

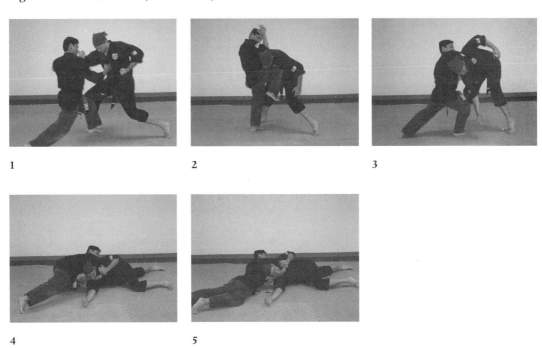

1          2          3

4          5

1. When a punch is delivered, move your body inside by stepping your left leg in. Place your foot closer to their right foot and block

their punch with your left forearm from the inside out, simultaneously punching them with your right fist straight to their solar plexus. Note that you are actually moving at a forty-five-degree angle, slightly perpendicular to your opponent's body.

2.  Slide your right arm upward and at the same time elbow their chest with your right elbow. Raise your right knee up to their face and simultaneously drop your right elbow down, crunching your opponent's head between your elbow and your knee.

3.  Drop your knee down and wrap around your opponent's neck with your right arm locking the neck. When the neck is locked, use your left hand to push their right shoulder down towards their left side so that your right hand can hold your left hand wrist.

4.  Maintain the hand lock to their neck and extend your right leg far behind you, dropping your opponent on the ground. Your opponent's shoulder is now smashed to the floor.

5.  Maintain your hand lock, lie on your stomach and apply pressure to their neck by tightening up the lock and moving slightly to your right side by twisting your upper body. Applying greater force breaks your opponent's neck. Great care must be taken to avoid irreparable harm.

**Figure 15-4-9:** *Pecahan selak mati* (**deadly locked variation one**).

1.  When a punch is delivered, move your body inside by stepping your left leg in and placing your foot closer to their right foot. Block their punch with your left forearm from the inside out and simultaneously punch them with your right fist straight to their solar plexus. Note that you are actually moving at a forty-five-degree angle, slightly perpendicular to your opponent's body.

1  2  3

4  5  6

2. Slide your right arm upward, elbowing their chest with your right elbow and raising your right knee up to their face. Simultaneously drop your right elbow down, crunching your opponent's head between your elbow and your knee.

3. Push your opponent's head down underneath your right leg and squeeze their head with your two legs.

4. Grab their belt or left arm from behind and simultaneously hold on to their right arm.

5. Drop yourself as if you are making a backward roll and pull your opponent's body down, directing their body to your left side.

6. Maintain your leg lock tightly to their head. When your opponent is on their back, your legs should already be locking their head and your right hand holding their right arm. Apply pressure

to their right arm by pulling down their wrist. This will put pain on their elbow, which is already placed on your stomach. Apply pain to their neck by squeezing your two-leg lock on their neck. Locking your feet, which are crossing each other, enhances the squeezing.

**Figure 15-4-10:** *Patah julang* (**broken boost**).

1            2            3

4            5            6

1. When a punch is delivered, move your right foot back in a clockwise direction at a ninety-degree angle and simultaneously catch your opponent's right wrist with your hands. When catching their hand, it is important to place your left hand under their wrist and your right hand above their wrist.

2. Pivot your body to your left and concurrently swing your oppo-

nent's right arm, making a semicircle from a downward-up motion to your left side.

3.  Pivoting your body to your left and swinging their arm gives momentum to your right leg in order to easily execute a round-house kick to your opponent's chest.

4.  After the kick to their chest with your right leg, position your leg to your left. Simultaneously placing their arm on your left side, going over your head and rotating your body to face their back. Their arm is now on your right side.

5.  While holding their arm with both hands, use your left leg to pin down the back of their right knee, bringing them down on their knee. Balance your body using your right leg by using a low stance.

6.  Bend their right arm behind their lower back, placing their arm on your left lap, and pin their hand with their own back by pulling their body down closer to you, using your right hand to grab their throat. Stretch their body back, exposing their neck and smashing their neck or upper chest with your left elbow.

**Figure 15-4-11:** *Pecahan patah julang* (**variation one**).

1.  When a punch is delivered, move your right foot back in a clockwise direction at a ninety-degree angle and simultaneously catch your opponent's right hand wrist with your hands. When catching their hand, it is important to place your left hand underneath their wrist and your right hand above their wrist.

2.  Pivot your body to your left and concurrently swing your opponent's right arm, making a semicircle from a downward-up motion to your left side.

1

2

3

4

3.  Pivoting your body to your left and swinging their arm gives momentum to your right leg in order to easily execute a round-house kick to your opponent's chest.

4.  Immediately after the kick to their chest with your right leg, position your leg to your left. Simultaneously place their arm on your left side, going over your head and rotating your body facing their back. Their arm is now on your right side.

5.  While holding their arm with both hands, use your left leg to pin down their back right knee, bringing them down on their knee. Balance your body using your right leg by using a low stance.

**5**

**6**

**7**

**8**

6.  Switch their arm to your right hand, making a wristlock and pushing your opponent's arm in front of you to their right side. Apply pressure on their right wrist to maintain control.

7.  Step forward with your left leg, at the same time pushing your opponent's upper arm with your left hand forward, making them go down to the ground.

8.  When your opponent is on the ground, step your left leg over their right arm, locking their elbow and dropping your right knee to the ground to secure your seating. Maintain the wristlock to control their body movement. Pushing their arm forward will break their elbow. Great care must be taken to avoid irreparable harm.

**Figure 15-4-12:** *Pasak mati* (deadly anchor).

1. When the opponent delivers their punch, move your right leg back by positioning yourself at about 135 degrees, and simultaneously block their punch with your left forearm from the outside in.

2. Lean forward and rotate slightly to your left and simultaneously swing your right arm, bending your opponent's right elbow from the inside out using your left arm to push their right forearm down, assist your right arm in executing the chicken-wing lock on your opponent's right arm.

3. Bend their arm behind their right shoulder and lock their right arm using your left arm. Push their shoulder downward by lowering your body with a low horse stance.

4. Lock their right arm with your left arm and step your right leg forward, close to your opponent's head, and strike the back of their neck with your right hand. Push your opponent's body down by sitting down on the floor.

5. Before your opponent falls on the floor, lift up your left leg and wrap it around their shoulder. Lock their right arm and execute a chicken-wing lock. Immediately push them down to the floor with your left leg and apply your body weight to push them down. Sit on the floor and maintain the arm lock. Grab their left arm and apply another chicken-wing lock. Pull the lock up to put pressure and pain on their upper body.

1

2

3

4

5

## ☀ Super Combat Techniques and Variations

*Serangan maut,* sometimes called *serangan harimau* or super combat techniques, apply fewer body lock movements. The super combat concept applies strikes, knees, kicks, elbows, takedowns, uppercuts, crosses, jabs, and hits to vital body parts. The defender protects them self by blocking and attacking the opponent at the same time. The strikes should be continuous, and generally the combat execution should be completed in two to four seconds.

There are twenty-one recorded basic replicas of super combat techniques. Each technique can be broken down into many different variations. The following figures show examples of combat techniques and variations. The techniques shown are not in any particular order.

**Figure 15-5-1: Patah dayong nasi hangit (broken paddle overcooked rice).**

1. The opponent is ready to deliver their punch.

2. When the punch is delivered, step outside at a forty-five-degree angle and lean to your left. Simultaneously position both of your arms to your left side ready to strike their back.

3. Pivot slightly to your right, and strike their lower back with your hands.

4. Grab their right wrist with your right hand and their chin, hair, forehead, or throat with your left while positioning your left leg ready to sweep their right leg.

5. Simultaneously pull them back and sweep their right leg with your left.

1

2

3

4

5

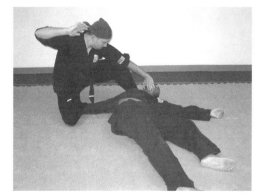

6

6. Drop your body down closer to their head above their right shoulder, and pin their right arm underneath your right knee. Using your left hand, lift up their chin, and strike their throat with your right hand.

**Figure 15-5-2:** *Pecahan patah dayong nasi hangit* (**variation one**).

1

2

3

4

1. The opponent is ready to deliver their punch.

2. Step outside and forward slightly to your left side with your left leg, and lean forward while your left hand pushes their right pelvis, and your right hand hooks their right knee from underneath.

3. Maintain grabbing their right leg and continue pushing them down, following them closely when they fall.

4.  Pull their right leg up with your right hand and execute a straight-down kick to their neck, chin, or face.

**Figure 15-5-3:** *Pecahan patah dayong nasi hangit* (**variation two**).

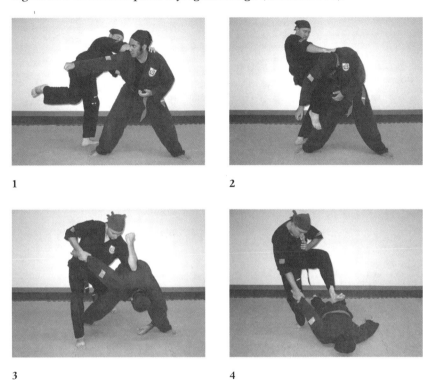

1

2

3

4

1.  Step outside at a forty-five-degree angle with your left leg and simultaneously reach your opponent's left shoulder with your right hand for balancing maneuver.

2.  Raise your right leg and knee straight to their right ribs.

3.  Immediately after kneeing, grab their right hand with your right hand and put your right leg in front of them on their right side. Rotate your body to your right side and elbow their back with your left arm.

4.    Execute a straight-down kick to their head, neck, or back.

**Figure 15-5-4:** *Kuda gila* (**crazy horse**).

1

2

3

4

5

1.    When the opponent delivers their punch, step outside at forty-five-degree angle with your left leg, and concurrently execute a kick with your right leg to their right ribs.

2.    Rotate your body in a clockwise direction and use both arms to push their right arm up, simultaneously sweeping their right leg in front of them.

3.    As they are about to fall back, rotate your body in a clockwise direction and execute a back kick to their lower back with your right leg.

4. Continue your body rotation and kick their head with your left leg.

5. Follow them to the floor by dropping your left knee to their right shoulder or throat and your right knee to their right ribs. Strike their neck or face with both of your hands.

**Figure 15-5-5:** *Lipat gayong pangku kawah pecah kawah* (**cross support broken crater**).

1              2              3

4              5

1. Your opponent is ready to deliver their punch.

2. Step your left leg inside at a forty-five-degree angle and simultaneously cross both of your arms (right arm on top), grabbing their shoulders. Your arms should push their shoulders back when making contact so that they lose their balance.

3. Pull your left hand down towards your left side and push your right forearm to their neck down toward your right side, at the same time raising your right leg and knee their lower back. These movements will make your opponent rotate their body in a clockwise direction. Caution should be taken—if too much force is used it may break their backbone.

4. Drop their body down and position their lower back on your right knee. This drop is dangerous and could break their backbone—great care must be taken to avoid irreparable harm. Maintain the grab on their neck and strike or elbow their upper chest with your left arm.

5. Abruptly drop their body to the ground by pushing their body down with your arms and pulling back your right knee. Execute a down-kick with your right leg or both legs to their face, upper chest, or abdomen.

**Figure 15-5-6:** *Patah halu pangku mayat*
**(broken path supporting corpse).**

1. Your opponent is ready to deliver their punch.

2. Step your body out of their line of force and grab their hair, forehead, or nose from the top with your left hand and pull them back. Simultaneously position your right leg ready to execute a straight-down pin to the back of their right knee.

3. Continue pulling their head down and execute the pin-down kick with your right foot on the back of their right knee.

4. Stretch their back downward in front of you, opening their neck and upper chest, and elbow their neck with your right arm.

1

3

4

**Figure 15-5-7:** *Kipas gayong tembi gayong selak gayong*
(**fanning locked elbow**).

1. When a punch is delivered, move your right foot forward and
   inside at forty-five-degree angle, and simultaneously grab their
   right hand with your left hand. Strike their neck or face with your
   right hand.

2. Push them back and downward with your hands, and sweep their
   right leg with your right leg.

3. Maintain the grip on their right hand and execute a kick straight
   to their jaw or face.

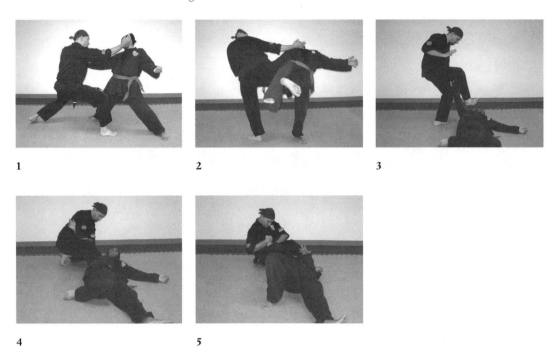

1

2

3

4

5

4. Lock their right hand with your right leg by sliding your foot under and behind their neck.

5. Sit on the floor and put your left leg in front of their throat, cross-locking both of your feet. Maintain the grip on their right hand with both of your hands, and put the pressure and pain on their upper body and head by straightening your right leg slowly. Care should be taken not to jerk your right leg abruptly, for it may dislocate their right shoulder joint and break their elbow.

**Figure 15-5-8:** *Buah sepukai siku temi patah dayong selak mati*
(stormy elbow broken paddle deadly locked).

1

2

3

4

1.  Move your left leg inside at forty-five-degree angle, and use your left palm to strike their chin or face in an upward motion.

2.  Rotate your body in a clockwise direction and elbow their solar plexus with your right elbow.

3.  Push their head in a forward-down motion with your right hand and simultaneously sweep their left leg in front of you, using your right leg.

4.  Execute a straight-down kick to their head or back using your right leg.

## ☼ Pukulan (Striking)

Another technique comparable to the super combat category is *puku-lan*. *Pukulan* is essentially a derivative of *asas elakkan* and *asas gerakkan* (basic blocks and basic movement) with variations and multiple follow-ups striking and pounding. Unlike b*uah tapak* (fruits), which applies body locking, *pukulan* does not. Super combat falls in between *puku-lan* and *buah tapak*. *Pukulan* consists entirely of striking and kicking. In the English language, *pukulan* simply means smacking or beating.

There are twenty-one basic replicas of *pukulan* techniques. Each technique can be broken down into many different variations. The following figures show examples of *pukulan* techniques. The techniques shown are not in any particular order.

**Figure 15-6-1: Technique One.**

1

2

3

4

5

1. Step outside with your left foot and strike your opponent's right ribs with your left hand. It is important to maintain a low horse stance so that you will not get hit to your face with their punch.

2. Follow up the strike with your right hand to their right ribs.

3. Follow up the strike again with a kick to their ribs with your right leg.

4. Immediately after the kick, pin down their right knee with your right foot.

5. Execute a front kick or an x-kick on their back with your left leg.

**Figure 15-6-2: Technique Two.**

1                              2                              3

1. Step forward and outside with your left foot, and use your right hand to hold the back of their neck for balance. Immediately raise your right knee straight to your opponent's right ribs.

2. With the same leg, sweep their right leg and pull them down.

3. Execute a straight-down kick to their face.

**Figure 15-6-3: Technique Three.**

1

2

3

4

5

6

1.  Step forward and inside with your left leg, and rotate your body in a clockwise direction.

2.  Maintain your low position (knee on ground) and strike your opponent's right ribs with your right hand.

3.  Rotate to your left side and strike their left ribs with your left hand.

4.  Move your left foot to your left side and execute a straight punch to their abdomen or groin.

5.  Stand up and simultaneously kick their groin with your right leg.

6.  Immediately follow up the kick with a sidekick to their solar plexus using your right leg.

**Figure 15-6-4:  Technique Four.**

1                              2                              3

1.  Step forward and inside with your left foot, and use your left palm to strike their face upward.

2.  Follow up the strike with a punch straight to their solar plexus with your right hand.

3.  Kneel down and punch their groin with your left hand.

**Figure 15-6-5: Technique Five.**

1

2

3

4

1. Step forward and inside with your left foot, and immediately kick forward to their left thigh or knee.

2. Follow up the kick with another kick to their groin with your right leg.

3. Hold the back of their neck with both of your hands.

4. Raise your left knee straight to their face.

**Figure 15-6-6: Technique Six.**

1

2

3

4

1.   Step your left foot slightly to your left and move your right foot for-
     ward, striking their right ribs with your right hand.

2.   Move your left foot forward and rotate your body to your right,
     striking their neck with both of your hands.

3.   Grab their upper shoulder and pull them down.

4.   Step back and position yourself above their head level. Poke their
     eyes with your fingers or slap downward to their face with both
     of your hands.

**Figure 15-6-7: Technique Seven.**

1                   2                   3

1. Step forward and inside with your right foot at a forty-five-degree angle, and kick your opponent's groin with your left foot.

2. Drop your body down to the floor on your right side as if you are about to do a push-up and immediately raise your right leg and execute a back kick to their abdomen.

3. Rotate your body to your right side and rise up and execute a roundhouse kick to your opponent's chest.

## ☀ Knife Techniques and Variations

There are twenty-one recorded *pisau* (knife) combat disarming techniques. Each technique can further be broken down into many different *pecahan* (variations). Including the *pecahan,* the movement is limitless. For point of reference, twenty-one techniques were thoroughly chosen as the base replica. The following figures show examples of knife disarming techniques and some variations. The techniques shown are not in any particular order.

**Figure 15-7-1: Technique One.**

1

2

3

4

1. Your opponent is ready to deliver a straight-thrust stab to your abdomen.

2. Move your right leg back at almost a 180-degree angle and catch their right wrist with both of your hands. (Note that your left hand is on the outside when grabbing and your right hand is on the inside closer to you.)

3. Rotate your body to your left and swing the wristlock to your left side, pulling them down.

4. Pin their arm with your right knee and grab the knife.

**Figure 15-7-2: Technique one variation.**

1                              2                              3

1.  When a knife stab to your abdomen is executed, move your right leg back at a 180-degree angle and catch their right wrist with your hands from the top. Slightly squeeze their arm with your upper left arm, locking their right arm under your left armpit.

2.  Using your body weight, drop your body by pushing their right elbow down while pulling the wristlock upward.

3.  Pull their right arm up toward your right side and move your body slightly forward toward their head in a downward motion. This will put pressure and pain on their shoulder.

**Figure 15-7-3:  Technique two.**

1                              2                              3

1. When your opponent's stab is executed, lean your body to the right and rotate your upper body in a clockwise direction. Simultaneously grab their right wrist with your right hand and block their hand with your left forearm at their right elbow.

2. Using your body weight and your left forearm, push their right elbow forward and down to the floor while you step forward with your left leg.

3. Put your left knee on the back of their right shoulder and their right arm on top of the right side of your right thigh. Put pressure on their shoulder by putting your body weight on your left knee. Care should be taken not to push too hard on their shoulder, for it might dislocate the shoulder joint.

**Figure 15-7-4:  Technique three.**

1                    2                    3

4                    5

1. When the stab comes, move your right leg back at an angle of ninety degrees and simultaneously grab their right wrist with your hands.

2. Pivot your body to your left, and at the same time swing their right arm to your left in a downward-up motion.

3. Concurrently kick their abdomen or chest with your right leg.

4. Pin down the back of their knee with your right leg, and grab their neck with your right hand.

5. Swing their head down to the floor behind your left foot, and maintain the choke to their neck.

**Figure 15-7-5: Technique three variation.**

1

2

3

4

1. When your opponent's stab comes, move your right leg back at an angle of ninety degrees and simultaneously grab their right wrist with your hands.

2. Pivot your body to your left and at the same time swing their right arm to your left in a downward up motion. Concurrently kick their abdomen or chest with your right leg.

3. After the kick, put your leg behind you and grab their right elbow with your right hand and pull their elbow down to the floor.

4. Pin their right shoulder with your right knee and lock their right arm. Use your weight to put pressure and pain on their elbow and shoulder.

**Figure 15-7-6:  Technique four.**

1

2

3

4

1.  Your opponent is ready to stab your head from the top.

2.  Move your left leg outside and raise your hands to block their right forearm at a forty-five-degree angle.

3.  Grip their right wrist with your left hand, and push their arm back with your hand while sweeping their right leg with your right leg.

4.  Pin their right arm with your right knee and grab the knife.

**Figure 15-7-7:  Technique four variation.**

1

2

3

4

5

1.  Step your left leg outside at a forty-five-degree angle and raise both of your arms, crossing each other, and block their downward stabbing motion. It is important that the block be slightly to your right and not above your head. Blocking the knife above

your head can be very dangerous because the knife used could be longer than you expected and it could stab your head.

2.  This block is actually a redirection of their stabbing motion, not a static block. As soon as the contact is made to their forearm, swing their arm in a down-up motion from your right to your left side in a circular motion while pivoting your body to your left.

3.  Grip their hand with your hands and deliver a kick to their chest or abdomen.

4.  Maintain holding their right arm and wrap your left leg around their right shoulder. Continue the chicken-wing lock with your left leg and use your body weight to push their body down to the floor. Caution should be taken as you push their body down because too great of a force might dislocate their shoulder joint.

5.  Grab the knife and maintain the lock on their shoulder and wrist-lock on their hand with your left hand.

**Figure 15-7-8: Technique five.**

1.  Move your right leg forward and inside while crossing both of your arms (left hand underneath right hand), and block the stabbing motion slightly to your left side. Do not do a static block and do not block perpendicular to the stabbing motion. The knife may be longer then you think, and you may get stabbed.

2.  As you make contact with their arm, swing their hand outside to your left with your left hand, and grab the back of their neck with your right hand. Swing their upper body to your left side in a down-up motion.

1          2          3

4          5

3.  The image shows your continuing swing motion to your left.

4.  Maintain holding their right hand and keep pushing their body until it is down on the floor.

5.  Pin their right arm by putting your right knee straight down on their elbow. Use your body weight to put pressure and pain on their elbow. Caution must be taken when putting your weight on the elbow. Too much pressure will dislocate the shoulder joint.

**Figure 15-7-9: Technique six.**

1.  When the opponent is executing the stab in a reverse motion to your neck, step your right leg forward and inside, and block their right arm with your right arm using a forward-down motion.

1

2

3

4

2. Using your left hand, push their right elbow down.

3. Step your left leg forward and push their elbow down.

4. Execute a wristlock on their right hand with your hands. Put pressure and pain by pushing the wristlock straight down.

## ☀ Simbat (Short Staff) Techniques

A *simbat*, sometimes called *simbat suk,* is a short stick of about three-and-a-half-feet in length. The diameter of the stick is about one-and-a-half- to two-inches. Normally, a *rattan* is used as a *simbat* because of its resistance and flexibility.

There are twenty-one recorded basic *simbat* techniques chosen as the base replica. Each technique can be further broken down into many different *pecahan* (variations). The following figures show examples of *simbat* techniques. The techniques shown are not in any particular order.

**Figure 15-8-1: Technique one.**

1

2

3

4

5

1.  Your opponent is ready to swing the *simbat* to your head from the top.

2.  Move your right leg forward, inside and close to them, and rotate your body in a counter clockwise direction. Open both of your arms to catch both of theirs as they swing the *simbat* towards you.

3.  Grab both of their forearms with your arms as if you want to hug their arms, and use your right shoulder to put pressure and

pain on both of their elbows by pushing their forearms down. Caution should be taken not to jerk these arm locks too hard or you might break their elbows.

4. Maintain the grab on their forearms using your right arm and grab their *simbat* with your left hand by pulling it down.

5. Hit their lower body with the *simbat*.

**Figure 15-8-2: Technique two.**

1

2

3

4

5

1. Your opponent is about to swing the *simbat* to your left side.

2. Move your right leg forward and inside, and rotate your body in a counter-clockwise direction. Open both of your arms to catch and jam their swing arms.

3.  Wrap your right hand around their forearms from the bottom. Lean slightly forward and position your right leg back, blocking both of their legs to move forward. Using your hips, pull both of forearms down, slamming them to the ground.

4.  Step downward on the right forearm to detach the *simbat* from their hand.

5.  With the *simbat*, strike their head or upper body.

**Figure 15-8-3: Technique three.**

1.  Your opponent is about to thrust the *simbat* straight to your abdomen.

2.  Step your left foot slightly forward and move your right leg back at a ninety-degree angle, simultaneously grabbing the *simbat* with both hands (right hand in front of the *simbat* and left hand in the middle between their two hands).

3.  Pin down their right knee with your left leg and pull the *simbat* slightly behind them.

4.  Twist the *simbat* in a counter-clockwise direction from their front over their shoulder to their back, making them lose their *simbat* grip and fall down.

5.  Take control of the *simbat* and strike their head or upper body.

1

2

3

4

5

**Figure 15-8-4: Technique four.**

1

2

3

4

5

1. Your opponent is about to swing the simbat at your left side.

2. Move forward with your right leg and rotate your body in a counter-clockwise direction standing closer to the front of their body. Simultaneously use your left palm to jam their forearms, and position your right elbow to strike their face.

3. Step your right foot slightly to your right. At the same time elbow their face with your right elbow while holding their *simbat* with your left hand.

4. Grab the *simbat* and strike their head.

5. Continue the strike to the head or upper body.

**Figure 15-8-5: Technique five.**

1

2

3

4

1. Your opponent is about to swing the *simbat* at your right side.

2. Move forward with your left leg and rotate your body in a clockwise direction, positioning yourself closer and in front of them so that you can jam their swinging arms.

3. Using your left arm and upper left body, hug and grab their arms tightly and twist their arms in front of you, making them lose balance and fall to the ground.

4. Maintain the arm lock with your left hand and grab the *simbat*. Rotate your body to the right side and thrust the *simbat* straight to their body.

**Figure 15-8-6: Technique six.**

1

2

3

4

5

1.  Your opponent is about to thrust the *simbat* straight to your abdomen.

2.  Step your left foot slightly forward and move your right leg back at a ninety-degree angle, simultaneously grabbing and jamming the *simbat* with both hands (right hand in front of the *simbat* and left hand in the middle between their two hands).

3.  Pin down their right knee with your left leg and pull the *simbat* slightly back.

4.  Using your left leg, step behind them and insert their head inside your arm opening.

5.  Pull the *simbat* back and up behind them, and choke their throat with the *simbat*.

**Figure 15-8-7: Technique seven.**

1

2

3

4

1.  When the opponent swings their *simbat* to your left side, lean slightly back, stepping away from the *simbat* and letting the *simbat* pass in front of you.

2.  When the opponent comes back and swings the *simbat* on the opposite side, move closer to them by stepping your left foot in front of them. Jam the swing with your left arm and the *simbat* with your right arm.

3.  Using the momentum of their swing force, step your left leg further to your left and throw them in front of you.

4.  Pin their shoulder or head with your left knee, grab the *simbat*, and strike their upper body.

## ☀ Long Stick Techniques

Long stick in Malay is *kayu panjang*. The diameter of the long stick is about one- to one-and-a-half-inches. Normally, a *rattan* is used because of its resistance and flexibility. The length of *kayu* used is commonly about the same as your height or slightly taller.

There are twenty-one recorded basic *kayu* combat techniques chosen as the base replica. Each technique can further be broken down into many different *pecahan* (variations). The following images show examples of *kayu* techniques. The techniques shown are not in any particular order.

**Figure 15-9-1: Technique one.**

1. Your opponent is about to strike your head with their *kayu*.

2. Move your right leg forward and inside at a forty-five-degree angle, and simultaneously swing your *kayu* inside out, redirecting their arms and the *kayu's* line of force.

3. Continue the swing until it gets to shoulder level.

4. Thrust your *kayu* straight to the right side of their head, hooking their neck down and pulling down.

5. Continue pulling your *kayu* down making their head spin in a downward-clockwise motion.

6. Finish the spin until they fall down to the ground, close to your feet, and execute the downward-thrust motion with your *kayu* to their face, head, or upper body.

1

2

3

4

5

6

**Figure 15-9-2: Technique two.**

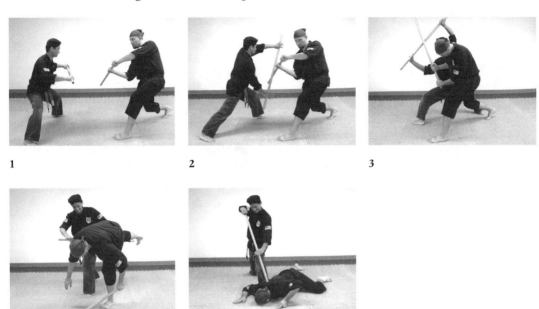

1

2

3

4

5

1. Your opponent is ready to strike your left side with a down up motion.

2. Step your left foot outside at a forty-five degree angle and block your opponent's *kayu* with your left hand above and right hand below.

3. Step forward with your right leg to your opponent's right side and simultaneously swing your *kayu* upward counter clockwise.

4. Using the left end side of your *kayu*, hook your opponent's right leg and swing the *kayu* behind you making your opponent fall forward to the ground.

5. Using the left end side of your *kayu*, thrust downward to your opponent's upper back.

**Figure 15-9-3: Technique three.**

1

2

3

4

1.  When the opponent tries to strike the *kayu* to your head, move your left leg forward and outside of the force line, blocking their upward strike with your kayu horizontally.

2.  Extend both of your arms forward and insert their head in the center of your arm opening, and pull their head closer to you. Simultaneously raise your right leg and knee straight to their right ribs.

3.  Tighten up the choke with your *kayu* and your arms.

4.  Pin their right knee with your right foot and place your right knee on their lower back. Push slightly forward and pull their head

backward, twisting slightly to your left. Caution should be taken not to jerk quickly, for this might break their spine.

**Figure 15-9-4: Technique four.**

1

2

3

4

1. When your opponent tries to strike your head with their *kayu,* step outside with your left leg at a forty-five-degree angle and swing your *kayu* on the right side to his abdomen.

2. Rotate your body in a clockwise direction and swing your *kayu* on your left side to the back of their neck or head.

3. Simultaneously sweep their right leg from the front, making them fall on their stomach.

4. Execute a downward thrust with your *kayu,* straight to their back.

**Figure 15-9-5:  Technique five.**

1

2

3

4

5

1.  When your opponent tries to strike your right side, block your right side vertically with your *kayu*.

2.  Pivot your body to your left side and simultaneously make a big swing with your *kayu* on your left side.

3.  Continue swinging the *kayu* into a low position by sitting on your knee.

4.  Execute a thrust straight to their abdomen with your *kayu*.

5.  As they fall down, swing your *kayu* on your left side straight into their groin.

**Figure 15-9-6: Technique six.**

1

2

3

4

5

6

1.  When your opponent tries to strike your head with their *kayu,* step outside with your left leg at a forty-five-degree angle.

2.  Swing your *kayu* on the right side to their abdomen or upper body.

3.  Slide the *kayu* to the back of their neck, going underneath their upper arm, and grabbing their right hand with your right hand.

4.  Raise your right leg and kick straight to their chest or abdomen.

5.  Immediately after the kick to the abdomen, sweep their right leg with your right leg, and maintain the lock on their neck with your *kayu.*

6.  Put their right hand palm up and pin it with your right foot. Put pressure and pain on their arm, shoulder, and neck by pulling the *kayu* upward.

**Figure 15-9-7: Technique seven.**

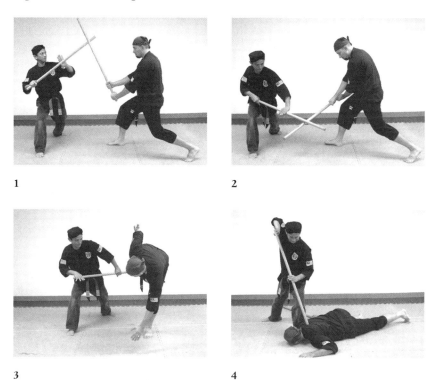

1

2

3

4

1.  When your opponent tries to strike your head with their *kayu,* step outside with your left leg at a forty-five-degree angle.

2.  Swing your *kayu* up from your left side, making contact on their *kayu,* and push their *kayu* down towards your right side in front of them.

3.  Continue the swing and hook their right foot from the front and lift up the foot with your *kayu.*

4.  When they fall down, thrust the *kayu* down straight on their back.

## ☀ Keris Techniques

The *keris* techniques shown in the following figures are techniques derived from *asas* (basic movements) and *pentas* (counter attack techniques) routines. Most basic block movements can be applied in any weapon technique with slight modifications depending on the weapons used. Generally, in any weapon defense, you have the alternative (if the opportunity allows) to simply strike at your opponent's weakest body parts such as the knee, neck, eyes, groin, veins, arteries, and solar plexus without catching or locking the opponent. However, in this section we will demonstrate the *keris* locking techniques that disarm the opponent. Most techniques apply joint locking, twisting, pulling, and pushing body parts at the weakest angle, and finally locking the opponent's body.

The updated curriculum recorded twenty-one known *keris* disarming base replica techniques. Each technique can further be broken down into many different variations. The following figures show examples of disarming techniques. The techniques shown are not in any particular order.

**Figure 15-10-1: Technique one.**

1.   Your opponent is about to thrust their *keris* weapon toward you.

2.   Step your right leg forward and inside at a forty-five-degree angle,

catch their right hand with your left hand, and strike their chin or face with your right hand.

3. Rotate your body to your left and step your right leg forward, simultaneously wrapping around their right hand by doing the figure-four lock.

4. Lift their right hand up, rotate your body 360 degrees to your right, and maintain the hand lock.

5. Lower your horse stance slightly and use your body weight to push them down to the floor.

6. Maintain the hand lock and put all of your body weight on their right side, applying pressure and pain by tightening up the figure-four lock. Caution should be taken not to jolt the hand lock back too forcefully—doing so might dislocate their shoulder.

**Figure 15-10-2: Technique two.**

1

2

3

4

1. Rotate your body at a 180-degree angle in a counter-clockwise direction. Simultaneously hold their right wrist with your left hand and elbow their right ribs with your right elbow.

2. Immediately after elbowing, move your right leg behind them and push their right hand along, sliding your right hand up behind their right shoulder and grabbing their chin.

3. Pull their upper body back by pulling their chin down with your right hand. Using their right hand, which you are already holding, pull down to put some pain and pressure on their neck and shoulder.

4. Use your right knee to push their right shoulder from behind. Put pressure on it by pulling their right hand down further. Caution should be taken not to jolt the right lock too much—doing so may dislocate their shoulder joint.

**Figure 15-10-3: Technique three.**

1                              2                              3

1. When your opponent's stab comes, move your left leg outside to your left side, rotate your body slightly in a clockwise direction, and drag your right leg behind you. Grab their right wrist with your right hand and simultaneously elbow their face with your left elbow.

2. Execute a figure-four lock. Make sure your left hand locks their right hand at their elbow joint.

3. Pin down their right knee with your left foot, and tighten up the figure-four arm lock by pushing their wrist down and lifting their elbow up with your left forearm. Do not jolt too much—doing so may rupture their elbow joint.

**Figure 15-10-4: Technique four.**

1

2

3

4

5

1.  When your opponent's stab comes, move your right leg back at an angle of ninety degrees and simultaneously grab their right wrist with your hands.

2.  Pivot your body to the left, swinging their right arm.

3.  Execute a kick with your right leg straight to their chest or abdomen.

4.  Before the kick is complete, reposition your right hand to push their right hand on your right side, and drop your right leg in front of you.

5.  Step forward with your left leg in front of you while your left hand pushes their triceps down, pinning their body down.

**Figure 15-10-5: Technique five.**

1

2

3

4

5

1.  Rotate your body counter-clockwise at 180 degrees and place your right leg in front of you, parallel to your opponent's right leg. At the same time, use both of your hands to catch their right hand by the wrist.

2.  Step forward with your left foot and raise their arm up. Apply a joint-lock on their wrist by pushing the wrist downward.

3.  Execute a kick with your right leg to their abdomen or chest.

4.  After the kick, wrap your leg around their right arm from the top and press downward, making them fall to the ground.

5.  Complete the right leg wrap around their right arm and sit down on the floor with your left knee up. Put pressure on their arm

and elbow by putting your weight on it. Caution should be taken not to put too much weight on their arm—doing so will rupture their elbow.

**Figure 15-10-6:  Technique six.**

1                                    2                                    3

4                                    5                                    6

1. When your opponent's stab comes, rotate your left foot counter clockwise direction at about 135 degrees and raise both arms to push your opponent's right arm upward in a circular motion.

2. Push your opponent's arm up and step your left foot behind their right hip.

3. Continue pushing their arm and wrap it around their neck. Use both of your arms to assist the wrapping motion of their arm.

4. Continue the arm wrapping motion and tighten up their arm around their neck.

5. Complete the wrapping and drag their upper body down to the floor and maintain the arm lock on their neck.

6. Use your left knee to apply pain and pressure on their upper body, neck, and shoulder.

**Figure 15-10-7: Technique seven.**

1                          2                          3

1. Step your left foot forward and outside, and simultaneously hold their right hand with your right hand. Elbow the right side of their face with your left elbow.

2. Wrap their neck with your left hand from the front of the neck and pull them back and downward.

3. Drop your right knee on the floor and place their upper body on your left knee. Maintain the neck lock with your left hand and put pain and pressure by pulling their right arm with your right hand, back toward your right side.

## ☀ Seni Siku (The Art of Elbowing)

*Seni siku* techniques use hands and elbows as your striking tool. Elbows are generally implemented when your opponent is at a closer distance. The following figures show seven elbow technique examples, not in any particular order.

**Figure 15-11-1: Technique one.**

1

2

3

4

1.  Move your left leg forward and inside at a forty-five-degree angle and simultaneously use your left hand to tiger-claw scratch their neck and chin in a down-up motion.

2.  Squat down and slightly rotate your body to your right side, and elbow your opponent's solar plexus or groin with your right elbow.

3.  Stand up and raise your right hand straight up, with your palm open, and strike their chin.

4.  Elbow their solar plexus with your right elbow.

**Figure 15-11-2:  Technique two.**

1                                2                                3

1.  Move your left leg forward and inside at a forty-five-degree angle, and simultaneously use both hands to punch straight to their solar plexus area.

2.  Immediately raise both arms and strike their jaw with open palms from bottom up.

3.  Drop both arms down and elbow their upper chest or collarbone with both of your elbows. If you are shorter than your opponent, elbow their solar plexus with both arms.

**Figure 15-11-3: Technique three.**

1

2

3

4

1. Move your left leg forward and inside at a forty-five-degree angle, and simultaneously use both hands to punch straight to their solar plexus.

2. Rotate your body to your right side and elbow their right ribs with your right elbow.

3. Reverse your body rotation and elbow their left ribs with your left elbow.

4. Step back with your left foot and concurrently elbow their upper chest or abdomen with both elbows.

**Figure 15-11-4:  Technique four.**

1

2

3

4

1. Move your left leg forward and inside at a forty-five-degree angle, and simultaneously elbow their jaw or face with your left elbow.

2. Squat down and elbow their groin with your left elbow.

3. Stand up and raise your left hand straight up with your palm open, and strike their chin.

4. Elbow their throat or upper chest with your left elbow again.

**Figure 15-11-5: Technique five.**

1                              2                              3

1. Move your right leg forward and outside, simultaneously elbowing their right ribs with your right elbow.

2. Reverse your right-elbow strike and hit their lower back.

3. Grab their shoulder or neck with your left hand and pull them down, exposing their chest, and elbow the chest with your right elbow.

**Figure 15-11-6: Technique six.**

1                              2                              3

1. Move your right leg forward and rotate your body in a counterclockwise direction, elbowing their left jaw with your right elbow.

2. Rotate your body in a clockwise direction and elbow their right jaw with your left elbow.

3. Rotate your body again in a counter-clockwise direction, and elbow their face with your right elbow.

**Figure 15-11-7: Technique seven.**

1                    2                    3

1. Move your left leg forward and inside at a forty-five-degree angle, and drop your right knee on the floor. Simultaneously swing your left hand from the outside in, straight to their groin, with an open palm or a strike.

2. Stand up and raise your right knee straight to their solar plexus, at the same time elbowing their chest with your right elbow.

3. Drop your right leg and elbow their upper back with your left elbow.

## ☀ Seni Seligi
## (The Art Knuckle Hand)

*Seligi* techniques use finger knuckles. The term finger knuckles refers to the knuckles on your upper fingers, rather than our normal understanding of what knuckles are. Figure 15-2-1 shows the finger knuckles.

**Figure 15-12-1: Finger knuckles.**

*Seligi* techniques target precise areas of your opponent's veins, arteries, muscles, and tendons. The strikes are lethal and great care must be taken when practicing these techniques. An intense strike can rupture the blood vessel and impede the blood circulation, which can cause extreme pain or even death. Figure 15-12-1 shows the *seligi* targets on the human body shown as dot points.

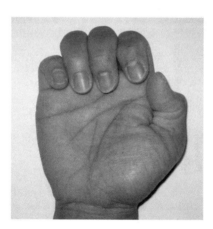 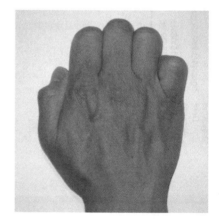

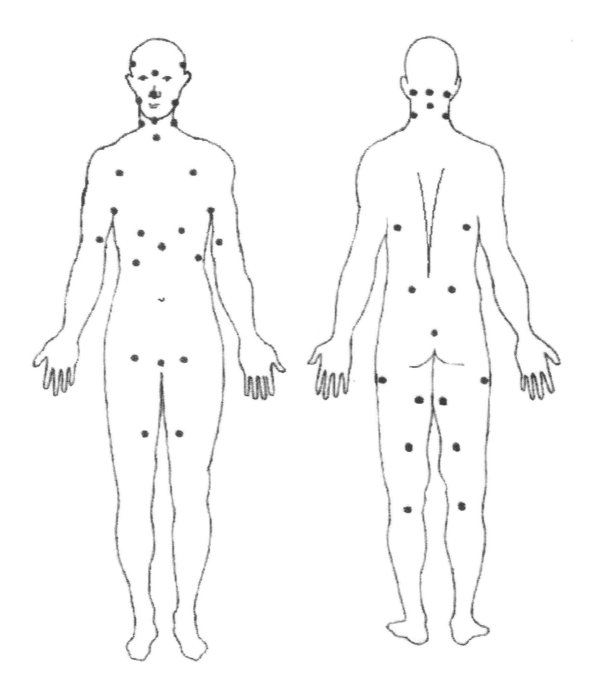

**Figure 15-12-2**

**Figure 15-12-3: Technique one.**

1

2

3

4

1. Move your left leg forward and inside at a forty-five-degree angle, and simultaneously strike straight to your opponent's throat with your left-hand knuckles.

2. Slide your left leg forward and rotate your body in a clockwise direction, positioning yourself to strike their left temple with your left hand.

3. Position your right leg behind them and strike their left temple with your left knuckles.

4. Using your right hand, strike the back of their neck.

**Figure 15-12-4:  Technique two.**

1

2

3

4

1.  Step your right foot forward and outside at a forty-five-degree angle, and strike your opponent's right temple with your right knuckles.

2.  Slide your right foot forward and rotate your body counter-clockwise, positioning yourself to strike again.

3.  Strike the back of their neck with your right knuckles.

4.  Strike their left temple with your left knuckles.

**Figure 15-12-5: Technique three.**

1

2

3

4

1. Move your left leg forward and inside at a forty-five-degree angle, and simultaneously strike straight to your opponent's throat with your left knuckles.

2. Slide your left foot forward and rotate your body clockwise.

3. Squat down and elbow their groin with your right elbow.

4. Stand up and raise your right hand straight up. Strike their chin with your right knuckles.

**Figure 15-12-6: Technique four.**

1

2

3

4

5

6

1.  Move your right foot forward and rotate your body counter-clockwise, positioning your back in front of your opponent.

2.  Using your right knuckles, strike their chin from bottom up.

3.  Squat down and elbow their groin with your left elbow.

4.  Stand up and raise your left hand straight up. Using your left knuckles, strike their chin.

5.  Push their left leg with your left foot.

6.  Using your right knuckles, strike their right thigh joint.

**Figure 15-12-7: Technique five.**

1                2                3

4            5

1. Step your right foot forward and outside at a forty-five-degree angle and strike your opponent's right temple with your right knuckles.

2. Slide your right foot in front of you, and rotate your body in a counter-clockwise direction positioning yourself ready to strike them again.

3. Execute a backhand slap with your left hand to the right side of their face.

4. Using your right knuckles, strike the back of their neck.

5. Using your left knuckles, strike their left kidney.

**Figure 15-12-8: Technique six.**

1                              2                              3

1. Step your left foot forward and inside at a forty-five-degree angle, and strike their solar plexus with your left knuckles.

2. Strike their throat immediately with your right knuckles.

3. Strike their nose or between their eyes with your knuckles.

**Figure 15-12-9:  Technique seven.**

1                              2

1. Move your left foot forward and inside, simultaneously kneel down, and strike their solar plexus with your left hand and their solar plexus with your right hand.

2. Rise up and strike their lower jaws with both of your hands.

# CHAPTER 16

# Adat Gelanggang—Training Center Rules and Regulations, Customs, Traditions, and Malay Culture

**Figure 16-1**

*Gayong* rules when in *gelanggang* (training hall):

- The hall in which you train *gayong* is called *gelanggang* in Malay. Traditionally, a fence around an open space outside surrounds the *gelanggang*.

- *Gayong* instructors are called *cikgu* in Malay. *Cikgu* means teacher—it is not a title.

- Before you begin training, you must pray or meditate. This is called *upacara buka gelanggang* (opening of training). This is the custom and it is mandatory. The goal is to clear your mind, remember the Almighty, concentrate, and focus on what you are about to do. Pray for the safety of all members and pray for all members, living and deceased. If your faith is Islam, you are required to recite the verse of *Al-Fatihah* one time, *Al-Ikhlas* eleven times, and *Selawat* three times.

- Before entering the *gelanggang* for training, take off your shoes and jewelry. This is for the safety of yourself and others.

- It is customary that you do not bow to the teacher. If you wish to greet the teacher, a simple handshake will suffice.

- If you are late, before joining the class sit on the floor near the training ground and meditate or pray on your own. When you have finished, greet the instructor by shaking hands. This is a gesture to ask permission to join the class and to acknowledge your presence.

- Be polite to each other at all times. Poor attitude will not be accepted. If you do not understand what you are required to do, ask the instructor.

- No sparring is allowed without the instructor's permission and supervision. Wearing safety equipment is highly recommended, although in traditional sparring these are nonexistent.

- Chest for females, groin for males, and shin protectors are allowed for safety.

- Swearing and smoking are strictly forbidden in the *gelanggang*. There should be no eating during class. Traditionally, water is not permitted, but because in the United States the weather is unpredictable and could drastically change within minutes, water is permitted to cool your body and to maintain energy.

- Always be aware of your safety and the safety of other members. Control your anger. Anger not only hurts you, but also hurts others.

- Before the class ends, everyone lines up in a circle or in multiple rows, sits down, and meditates or prays. You thank the Almighty for the safety of the members and ask that the knowledge gathered benefit all of us. This event is called *upacara tutup gelanggang* (closing of training), the same as the *upacara buka gelanggang.* If your faith is Islam, you are required to read the verse of *Al-Fatihah* one time, *Al-Ikhlas* eleven times, and *Selawat* three times.

- Before leaving the *gelanggang,* all students are required to greet each other by shaking hands. The first student on the left by the instructor will go around and greet everyone followed by the next student on the left and so on. The greeting indicates that all unintended actions or errors are forgiven and forgotten. This is also a gesture of brotherhood.

  In Malaysia, it is customary that males and females do not shake hands. A gesture, without touching, or a polite nod and smile will suffice. As far as mixed training, it is up to the individual. Each preference is honored with respect.

- In Malay culture, it is customary that when pointing at something, you use your thumb instead of your finger. Point using your right hand. The left hand is considered rude and is associated with hygiene purposes. Never point at something using your feet; it is considered rude.

- It is customary to remove one's shoes upon entering a Malaysian home.

- Never give something to someone using your left hand. Use your right hand or use both hands. The

**Fig 16-2**

same is true when receiving something. Use your right hand or both hands.

- It is uncommon for Malaysians to touch during conversations, especially if the other party is a member of the opposite sex. Malaysians consider it rude to pat or tap someone on the head.

- Malays, being Muslims, would find any gift containing pork or pig derivatives, dogs, and alcohol extremely offensive.

- Malays do not actually have surnames or family names. Instead, they adopt their father's first name. For example, Razali *bin* Salleh, which literally translated means Razali, son of Salleh. *Bin* means son of. Females use *binti* meaning daughter of. For example, Kalsom *binti* Meor Rahman.

- Many members of society were granted titles such as *dato* or *tan sri* by any one of Malaysia's sultans. Generally when a person has a title you address them with the title first. For example, *Dato* Meor Rahman.

- Age is wisdom. Elders are treated with respect. Most elderly Malays will be delighted to be greeted in the traditional Malay fashion by a light touching of the palms using both hands and then bring them to your chest. This signifies that you are greeting the person from your heart. When arriving or departing, it is best to avoid kissing and hugging.

# CHAPTER 17

# Silat Questions and Answers

1. **Where did silat originate?**

   Please see the section, *Brief History of Silat.*

2. **What is the main thing to look for when a student learns silat?**

   It depends upon the individual. Some practitioners continue searching for the ideal system, while others may want to build up mental toughness and self-assurance. Yet others many seek spiritual enlightenment. The bottom line, besides self-defense, is to become a better person. I strongly urge that when learning *silat* you try to recognize the essence of the art whole-heartedly, with your soul and spirit. Only then you will discover the true connotation of the *seni* within *silat*. Regardless of which art you learn, take the time to gain knowledge of, appreciate its history, and respect its culture and *adat* (traditions). We should acknowledge those parts of their identity.

3. **I have heard of many silat names. What are the main differences among all these silats?**

   Each has its own unique style, concepts, and philosophy. For example, silat *burung putih* is based on bird style. *Silat tjmande* is the water buffalo style. *Silat tjikalong* is the crane style. Of course, everyone is entitled to his or her own opinion. My opinion is that no single self-defense system fits everyone. Due to body size, individual capabilities, and physical condition, a certain self-defense may or may not be the right one for you. You have to feel natural and comfortable with the style you choose. The fact is that it is not so much the style but a combination of your knowledge of self-defense, its history and culture, your intelligence, and of course your kind heart. Strength or style alone cannot accomplish the goal. Remember, knowledge is power. Style is only a tool.

4.  **How many forms of silat are there in Malaysia and other parts of the world?**

In Malaysia there are more than 150 known *silat* styles.

Here are several *silat* names found in Malaysia:

| | |
|---|---|
| *Gayong* | *Cekak* |
| *Bunga* | *Pulut* |
| *Kelantan* | *Melayu* |
| *Kalimah* | *Jawa* |
| *Depowojo* | *Burung Puteh* |
| *Sendeng* | *Gerak Kilat* |
| *Keris Lok-9* | *Lincah* |

There is an unconfirmed report that in Indonesia alone there are about 400 known *silat* styles. There are a few in Singapore and the number in the Philippines is uncertain.

Recently *silat* has entered into sport competitions and has spread into the Western world, especially Europe.

5.  **Is *silat* only practiced in Malaysia, Indonesia, and Philippines?**

Most practitioners are from these countries. However, many *silats* now have spread to the Western world.

6. **Is *silat* influenced by Indonesian, Philippine, and Chinese arts, or is it in a category of its own?**

This is a very difficult question to answer. Actually, there is no known record on the exact origin of *silat*. However, history indicates that *silat* existed as far back as the seventh century A.D. History also denotes that there are some Chinese and Indian influences in *silat* and due to culture, religion, and geography, *silat* has evolved a great deal. Concrete proof describing the development of various *silats* is difficult to find. Because of this, each *silat* master has his own theories, stories, and legends describing the origins of his martial art.

There is a folk story in *silat*. Once there was a peasant woman who set out one day in the jungle to fetch some water. Upon arriving at the stream, she saw a confrontation between a tiger and a large bird that lasted for several hours, with both animals dying at the end of the fight. Later, several drunken villagers appeared and harassed the woman. Copying the movements from the tiger and the bird, she skillfully evaded her assailants. She then started to teach the movements to other inhabitants. Thus, a legendary female founded a defensive art.

7. **Is it true that in the old days it was difficult to learn *silat*, and that it was very secretive?**

Yes, it is true. In the old days, knowing *silat* completely meant that you had gained the knowledge of wisdom. You learned your true self and you learned the revelation of the unseen. You came closer to the Almighty and possessed a mystical knowledge and power. Great power comes with great responsibility; that is why teachers were very selective about whom they taught. They wanted the knowledge to be passed down to students they could trust, who had good moral and ethics, would use the knowledge wisely, and not become arrogant or egotistic. The knowledge should be taught to students who learn for the sake of learning and accept changes as part of the life process. There is an old Malay saying that uses the *sawah padi* plant (paddy plant) as an illustration:

*Ikut Resmi padi, semakin tunduk semakin berisi.*

More or less, this means that if you have accumulated vast knowledge, the more knowledge you receive, the more humble you should become. If you are unfamiliar with the paddy plant, when the paddy gets filled, the plant lowers or bows towards the ground. It is an excellent metaphor that all of us should contemplate.

### 8. Why has *silat* remained hidden from the Western world for so long compared to Japanese and Korean arts?

The Far East was not well known to the Western world. Some westerners do not know where Malaysia or Indonesia is located. To many westerners, *silat* is a soft movement or a dance. Another reason is that not many Indonesians or Malaysians came to the Western world until recently.

### 9. Who is responsible for bringing *gayong* in America?

**Figure 17-1**

I came to America in 1981, but did not teach *gayong* to anyone until 1989. I started to teach *gayong* privately to a black belt *hapkido* instructor, master Randy Stigall (figure 17-1). We began to exchange arts and learn from each other. That was when I started learning *hapkido*. It was a different and interesting experience for me, as well as for Randy.

While I was practicing *gayong* on my own, a Malaysian named *Cikgu* Sulaiman Shariff

started a small group on his own
in 1990 and became the founder
of *gayong* America. Initially he
started *gayong* in California and
then moved to Pennsylvania and
later to New Jersey. Unfortunately,
he went back to his homeland. Bill
Reed, under the supervision of
Sulaiman Shariff, currently main-

**Figure 17-2**

tains the *gayong* activity in New Jersey. (The photo in
figure 17-2 shows *Cikgu* Majid, *Cikgu* Sulaiman, and me
practicing *keris* techniques.)

My brother, *Cikgu* Sheikh Shamsul (figure 17-3)
assisted me in spreading *gayong* in Illinois while continuing his education here. He too went back to Malaysia.
I believe there was another person named *Cikgu*
Saharuddin Abdul Hamid who introduced *gayong* to
the southern part of Illinois. I knew him when we were
in Malaysia training together at *Kampong Pandan* Training Center in Kuala Lumpur, but I do not know much
about him beyond that. I believe he also went back to
Malaysia. There is a Native American martial art practitioner named Blaise Loong (figure 17-4) that learned
*gayong* from Malaysia. He traveled to Malaysia and met
*Dato* Meor Rahman. I do not know where he is, nor do
I know whether or not he teaches *gayong*.

**Figure 17-3**

Today, one of my senior students helps me to propagate *gayong* in the United States. His name is *Cikgu*
Joel Champ.

**Figure 17-4**

**Figure 17-5: Joel Champ.**

**10. At what age do most Malaysians begin studying the art?**

In the old times, children started to learn *silat* as early as nine or ten years old. Today, they usually begin during their teens. *Silat,* or martial arts in general, has become part of the school curriculum.

**11. Is the art an important part of the culture in its countries of origin?**

It has always been and will be forever. The art is demonstrated at wedding ceremonies, on Malaysian National Day, at culture shows, and sometimes at political events.

**12. Do all other forms of *silat* have as strong a Muslim influence as *gayong*?**

In Malaysia, the majority of *silat* practitioners are Muslim, but some follow the influence of Hinduism. This is true especially in Indonesia. Some *silat* practitioners in the Philippines are Christians.

**13. Are all *silat* masters Muslim?**

No. The *kuntao silat* style master that I know here in United States is a Christian. *Kuntao* itself is a Chinese art, of which the majority practices Buddhism. Some *serak silat* style masters here are Christians. I was told that the *serak silat* system was originally a Muslim system. In Malaysia, the majority of *silat* masters are Muslim.

**14. If I am a Christian, can I learn *silat*? What about the religious part of *silat*? Do I have to learn that, too?**

Religion is a personal preference. If you choose to learn *gayong,* the religion part of it will not be taught to you unless you choose to learn it. *Dato* Meor himself has taught *gayong* to several non-Muslim martial artists that came to see him. In *gayong,* religion becomes the guidance in life. Therefore, religion is used as direction and inspiration. One such example is the aikido grandmaster O'Sensei Ueshiba Morihei. He was a follower of Omoto-Kyu faith. He used religion in his martial art practices for total concentration and calmness. Most Chinese kung-fu masters blend the art with Buddhist practices, and some are Christians. In *gayong,* the majority of the practitioners are Muslim. Non-Muslim practitioners have started to appear.

It is up to the individual to blend religion with their martial art practice. Islam teaches tolerance and there is no compulsion in religion.

"To you your religion, and to me my religion." (109:6)

"There is no compulsion in religion." (2:256)

**15. Why is *ibu* (mother) so significant in *silat?***

Have you ever heard of this phrase? "Paradise lies at the feet of your mother." Metaphorically it means that if you intend to enter paradise, besides obeying the Creator, you must obey your mother for it was she who carried you in her womb for nine months, fed you, and nursed you until you became an able body. One of the many requirements in *silat* is to obey your parents. Disrespecting your parents means violating the vow of *silat.* True qualities of a *silat* practitioner are: to obey the Creator, parents, and teacher; to be humble; to have a good heart; to be sincere, loyal, righteous, and sincerely accept others as part of your life.

**16. You mentioned that in *gayong* under *adat istiadat gayong* we have to go through the *adat* before officially being accepted as a *gayong* student. Is that mandatory?**

The *adat* is mandatory if you are a Muslim. *Gayong* is rich with Malay cultures and traditions, respect, and *adab*. For a non-Muslim, the handshaking and the pledge suffice. *Dato* himself has accepted students that are non-Muslim.

**17. I heard that one of the many things done to test a *silat* practitioner's confidence is to make them walk on hot charcoal. Is this really true?**

Some *silats* will test their students with such things; others may not. Some of the tests include walking on hot charcoal or broken glass, bending hot metal with your teeth, and dipping your hands into hot boiling oil.

**18. What is a *pendekar*?**

*Pendekar* means fighter—a *silat* practitioner who has achieved full mastery of *silat*. It is believed that the word *pendekar* is derived from the *Minangkabau* expression *pandai akal* (intelligence). *Pendekar* also

Figure 17-6: Walk on hot charcoal.    Figure 17-7: Hot oil bath.

connotes a spiritualist and a leader who has obtained an understanding of true knowledge.

The title *pendekar* is difficult to receive, but not impossible. The title is generally given by the *mahaguru* (grandmaster), or the sultans of a particular province. You hear many people claiming that they are *pendekar.* They may be real or a scam.

**19. Are you a *pendekar*?**

No. I am not a *pendekar* nor am I a master of *gayong.* I am just a *silat* practitioner who wants to share and to propagate the Malay art of self-defense. The only title I received from the late *Mahaguru Dato* Meor Abdul Rahman was a title called *khalifah muda* (young caliph), in 1975 at Air Kuning, Taiping, Perak, Malaysia. Now I hold the title *ketua khalifah* (chief of caliph). The leader of Gayong Pusaka, *Cikgu* Majid Mat Isa has also given me the title of *khalifah besar sinar kebaktian.* (The caliph title indicates the degree of leadership.)

**20. In some arts they teach you artwork such as calligraphy and painting. Is there something similar to that?**

No, but some *silat* teachers may teach you how to read Arabic and study the Quran and the *Hadith* (Sayings of the Prophets).

**21. Is the *bunga*, or flowery dance, composed of set movements or self-created movements?**

At first, you will learn how to do a simple *silat* flower dance. Some *silats* call it *langkah one, langkah two,* and so on. Others may call it just *bunga* or *kembangan.* Once you have mastered these flower dances, you will automatically move without thinking, thus creating your own movement sets. In comparison, it is like learning *katas.* Once you have mastered the basic movements, you can actually create your own *kata.*

**22. Is there any other animal form involved in *silat* besides the tiger?**

Yes. For example, *silat burung putih* is based on bird style. *Silat tjmande* is the water buffalo style. *Silat tjikalong* is the crane style.

**23. Is there a *silat* form that is based only on the dragon or the tiger?**

I am not sure if there is a *silat* style based only on a dragon. As far as I am concerned there is none. However, there are many *silats* based on *harimau* (tiger) style.

**24. What are the healing arts involved in *silat*?**

A *silat* practitioner sometimes practices a massage therapy called *urut*. This *urut* is not just a normal massage. For the Muslim faith, the *urut* is done by your hands while extracting some appropriate verse of text from the Quran. If you are familiar with the Indian traditional *kerala* massage therapies, the *urut* is similar, with the exception of the verses extracted from the Quran.

Herbs are also widely used such as ginger, ginseng, and *jamu*. (*Jamu* is a family of herbs extracted from select tree roots and flowers.)

**25. How does the internal art of *silat* differ from the well-known Chinese internal arts?**

My understanding is that there are two levels of forces—*ilmu dalam* and *ilmu kebatinan*. *Ilmu dalam* is the internal energy or internal force. Everyone has internal energy. By controlling your *pernafasan* (breathing), you can develop a very strong body and mind control. This is the art of conditioning your body. So, developing internal force is relative.

*Ilmu kebatinan* is spiritual fulfillment. It is hidden and mysterious. *Kebatinan* is one who seeks to develop inner tranquility and an intuitive inner feeling through a method of self-submission. It is one who may experience intuitively the divine presence of the Almighty residing within the heart. Therefore, achieving *kebatinan* is quite difficult. Part of the *kebatinan* requires you to fast, meditate, and use mantras or *zikir* (chants) given to you by your teacher.

Chinese internal force is probably no different from *silat*. The method used to achieve that stage might be different. Like the Chinese monks who practice the martial art kung fu, their spirituality relates to Buddhism teachings. *Gayong* relates to Islam teachings. The objective is fundamentally the same—to develop noble character, good ethics, and a strong body and mind.

## 26. What are some weapons used in silat?

The weapons widely used in *silat* training are *pisau* (knife), *parang* (machete), short and long sticks, and *keris* (dagger). Other weapons such as *lawi ayam/kerambit* (a tiger claw-shaped knife), *sundang lipas* (a long sword shaped like a Viking sword), *badik* (a broad knife), *tekpi/djabang* (Sai weapon), and *cindai* (rope/veil) are used.

**Figure 17-8**

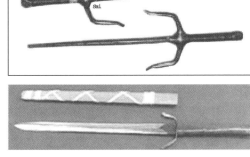

### 27. What are some of the unique characteristics found in Malay *silat?*

Besides being humble and having good ethics, Malay *silat* practitioners also practice the preservation of the *Malay adat istiadat* (Malay cultures and traditions), morality, *adab* (respect), and the use of religion as the inspiration, motivation, and guidance for high-quality behavior. There is an old saying, *"Hilang adat resam hilang bangsa,"* which more or less means that if you lose your culture, self values, and traditions, you have no self-identity. The legendary Malay warrior Hang Tuah also said, *"Takkan melayu hilang di dunia."* (Malay race, culture, tradition, and language shall not perish from this earth.)

### 28. What are the biggest differences between the more commonly known Indonesian or Dutch-Indonesian *silat* and Malay *silat?*

Each *silat* has its own unique concepts. In Indonesia, the art is generally referred to as *pentjak silat* and in Malaysia as *seni silat* or *silat seni.* The words *pencak silat* (*pencak* is the Malaysian spelling and *pentjak* is the Indonesian spelling) are still used in Malaysia, but not as often as in Indonesia. *Bersilat* is a verb that means, "to do *silat.*" While ninety-nine percent of the faith of Malay *silat* practitioners is Islam, Indonesian *silat* practitioners may be Muslim, Christian, or Hindu. Nevertheless, when referring to Indonesian or Malaysian *silat*, there is one common denominator—they all originate from a Malay ethnic group.

### 29. How is the training in the United States different from that of Malaysia?

From my experience and observations it differs in two aspects—physical training and legalistic issues.

The training in the United States is more equipped. We have all kinds of tools such as the head protection helmets used for free sparring, rubber knifes used for practicing knife techniques, weight training to develop strength and power, body protection equipment for contact sparring, and punching bags to help develop kicks. These are good for better training and safety. In Malaysia, most of the training centers do not have this equipment. The traditional way is used, because early practitioners did not have modern equipment.

As far as legality issues, in the United States you must have insurance for the school and students must sign legal documents agreeing not to take legal action if they get hurt before joining. Even then a school owner can be sued if things go wrong. In Malaysia, if you wish to learn *silat,* you pretty much understand the risks. You register as a member, go through the Malay *adat* ceremonies as a new student and you are in. No documents, no agreements, no insurance, and if you get hurt, fix it yourself. That is why they put their faith in the hands of the Almighty and pray for the safety of all members.

### 30. What do you hope to see as the future for *silat gayong* in the United States?

I would like to see *gayong* spread throughout United States in the right way. What I mean by this is that all *gayong* teachers should really be authentic *gayong* teachers, not teaching *gayong* without true knowledge. This can ruin the integrity of the *gayong* art. My plan is to pass down *gayong* to practitioners who truly want to study and to share the art with others.

### 31. There are currently four *gayong* organizations: Gayong Malaysia, Gayong Pusaka, Gayong Warisan, and Gayong PASAK Singapore. Is there any effort to consolidate them?

Each of us have different opinions, and all of them have some positive and negative aspects. In order to grow and to expand knowledge one must discover, evolve, and adapt to changes and new ideas without losing the originality and the uniqueness of the art. Each *gayong* organization has it own differences and similarities to others. No matter what these are, all organizations acknowledge the fact that the founder of *gayong* will always be *Dato* Meor Abdul Rahman.

Perhaps someday all of the *gayong* organizations will be united. Their goal is the same—to propagate *gayong*. Several efforts have been made to consolidate, and the process continues. With the will of the Almighty, it will occur. As said in a *gayong* poem:

> *Pecah gayong di dalam dulang,*
> *Dulang hanyut di lautan tujuh,*
> *Perpecahan gayong perpecahan sayang,*
> *Disatu masa balik bersatu dan teguh.*

Simply put, the separation of *gayong* is the separation of love, and one day all *gayong* will be unified.

**32. You mentioned earlier that there are several *gayong* organizations (Gayong Malaysia, Gayong Pusaka, Gayong Warisan, and Gayong PASAK). Which organization do you belong to?**

When I first joined *gayong* in 1973, there was only one *gayong* organization in Malaysia. Gayong PASAK is the same *gayong* except that it is in Singapore. Now that I am here in the United States, I am promoting *silat seni gayong,* which stands for all of the *gayong* organizations that claim *Dato* Meor Rahman as their *mahaguru*. The United States *Gayong* Federation (USGF) will promote

**Figure 17-9**

the original *silat seni gayong*. I honestly anticipate that other *gayong* organizations will acknowledge my proposition with open arms. After all, we are all under the same guru. I have practiced and learned under several instructors from these organizations such as *Cikgu* Majid (figure 17-9) and *Cikgu* Awang (figure 17-10). In 1978, I was in Taiping, Perak in Malaysia, learning *cindai* techniques from *Dato* Meor and his daughter *Cikgu* Siti Kalsom. I have also practiced knife and combat techniques with *Cikgu* Badek Ruzaman (now Gayong Warisan). To me, promoting *gayong* means promoting one *silat—silat seni gayong*. The *silat* I am acquainted with came from *Dato* Meor Rahman. So, I support all *gayong* who respectfully maintain *Dato* Meor Rahman as their *mahaguru*.

**Figure 17-10**

**Figure 17-11: From left, *Cikgu* Sani, the author, Kamisah and *Cikgu* Kalsom. 1978 in Taiping, Perak.**

**Figure 17-12:  The author and *Cikgu* Majid practicing *keris*, 1998 in Chicago, Illinois.**

### 33. Have you done any *silat* seminars in the United States? Do you associate yourself with other *silat* instructors or other *silat* organizations within the United States?

I did a *gayong* demo with my brother Shamsul at the *khoso ryu kempo* seminar in Sacramento, California in mid-1995. Since then I have been invited by Guru William De Thouars to join the *kuntao silat* seminar in Denver, Colorado. In 1997, *Cikgu* Majid came to the United States, brought by *Cikgu* Sulaiman Shariff to do seminars in Chicago, Miami, and Los Angeles. I have also been invited to do other *silat* demonstrations and seminars within the local area.

**Figure 17-13:** The author and Guru Victor De Thouars—*serak silat.*

Since then, I have made friends with several martial artists such as Guru William De Thouars *(kuntao silat),* Victor De Thouars *(serak silat),* Guru Jim Ingram *(mustika kuwitang silat),* Guru Stevan Plinck *(serak),* Guru Bob Olando *(kuntao),* Guru Dr. Andre KnutGraichen *(kuntao),* Guru Wayne Welsh *(kuntao), hapkido* instructor Randy Stigall, and *kosho ryu kempo* chief instructor Bruce Juchnik Hanshi. I am also affiliated with the Pentjak Silat USA organization.

**Figure 17-14:** The author and his *aikido* teacher, Judy Leppert *Sensei.*

### 34. How do you teach your *silat* class?

I prefer to teach and mingle with the class in a traditional way with a modern and scientific approach. We need to preserve the originality and the uniqueness of the art, but at the same time we need to evolve and open our minds to new

Figure 17-15: The author, his brother Shamsul, and Guru William De Thouars—*kuntao silat*.

Figure 17-16: The author, his brother Shamsul, and Bruce Juchnik Hanshi—*kosho ryu kempo*.

Figure 17-17: The author and Jon Ludwig *Sensei*—*kosho ryu kempo*.

Figure 17-18: From left, *Sifu* Ed Clingo (Chin Lin Pai), the author, Master Randy Stigall (*hapkido*), *Sifu* Mike Moi (*Chinese kung fu*), *Cikgu* Joel Champ.

possibilities and perspectives. Sometimes changes are unavoidable due to circumstances. Never limit your options and absorb the useful. Common sense is held above all, and education is the key to breaking barriers of ignorance.

Teachers should not, *"set themselves up as gurus to be worshiped. Teachers must ultimately discover and develop their own skills, the experiences and views of other teachers can be valuable."** 

*"A competent teacher presents information. A great teacher inspires."*** 

---

*\*Carol A. Wiley, Martial Arts Teachers on Teaching, 1995, p. xi*
*\*\*Ibid, p. xi*

CHAPTER *18*

# Gayong from an American Perspective

## Gayong in the eyes of Joel Champ

### My Journey into *Silat Seni Gayong*

I began training in *silat seni gayong* almost ten years ago. I was first introduced to the martial arts by my father David Champ. My father is a well-respected teacher in the martial arts who has a strong background in many arts including Chinese internal *gung-fu*, *kosho ryu kempo*, *hapkido*, *aiki-jitsu*, *silat*, *kuntao*, and *arnis*. He was instrumen-

**Figure 18-1**

tal in introducing me to various arts including *silat seni gayong* and to my teacher, *Cikgu* Shiekh Shamsuddin "Sam" Salim.

I met *Cikgu* Sam and his brother Shamsul in January of 1995 at my father's school in Lisle, Illinois. I was drawn to this rare art and became obsessed with learning more. I saw many great qualities in this art and saw it for its totality in training. It was very visually aesthetic in its movements and cultural intricacies, but it was the underlining philosophy and spiritual aspects that made me decide to solely train in and pursue this art. After our school closed, I followed *Cikgu* Sam to many locations where we would train: local parks, his house, park districts, gymnasiums, and finally to our current location at Shoshin Dojo in Westmont, Illinois.

My personal art has changed dramatically and I have found that one of the secrets of our art is that in order to grow in *silat seni gayong* you must be driven to learn. The traditional teacher will not just give you everything you want. You must research and inquire, investigate, and feel. This process will teach you not only about the inner core quality of *gayong,* but also about yourself and the world in which you live. The greatest struggle is the struggle to know oneself. It will show you that ultimately you will get what you put into it. On the surface, you learn a viable form of self-protection. As a *gayong pesilat,* you will be able to evade attacks and defend with a tuned arsenal of unarmed and armed tactics, as well as develop environmental- and self-awareness. But more deeply and importantly, you will develop humility, piety, compassion, bravery, confidence, rationality, and a strong spirit and honor. These are the true markings of a person who has gone beyond just the limited outward physical structure to a more inner self-exploration that has no limitations. While it is easy to teach punching and kicking, the goal of *silat seni gayong* is to teach the student to think swiftly, with common sense and rational thought and to have a strong will and spirit. This is most important, because brute strength does not win a fight. It is a calm mind that produces cunning and tactical strategy that does. *Mahaguru Dato* Meor Abdul Rahman won many challenges from his strong mind and spirit.

I would like to thank Almighty God for my many blessings. I am in debt to my teacher *Cikgu* Sam for sharing with me his culture and knowledge. I am also truly grateful to my parents, to my supportive wife Joanna, my son Dylan, and all of my teachers. My teachers include: my father *Sifu* David Champ, Master Randy Stigall *(hapkido),* Master Glen Gavin *(tae kwon do* and boxing), *Hanshi* Bruce Juchnik *(kosho ryu kempo),* Coach John O'Brien (boxing), Coach Dave Rogers (Thai boxing), *Sifu* Dion Riccardo (JKD), *Bapak* Willem DeThouras *(kuntao), Cikgu* Shamsul Salim *(silat seni gayong),* and most importantly my friend, brother, and teacher *Cikgu* Sam. Thank you for allowing me the freedom to grow. To all of my brothers and sisters in *silat seni gayong* and in the spirit of *Dato* Meor Abdul Rahman, I say, *"Zaaaatt!"*

# Gayong in the Eyes of Gene Scott, Jr.

When I took my first *gayong* lesson I noticed that it was very aggressive and combative by nature. A *gayong* practitioner does not want to fight, but when he does, it is total destruction; it is over and done.

I have been told many times that, "without the knife there is no *silat.*" After training in *gayong,* I have begun to learn the meaning of that phrase. Now I know why *gayong* is so aggressive and combative. Knife fighting is no game. You do not have time to sit back and wait to see what your opponent is going to do, or see if he is carrying a knife or other weapon.

Figure 18-2

When the fight is on, attack your opponent, and end the fight as quickly and safely as possible. This is what *gayong* is to me. It is about survival.

I have studied many other arts, one art being *jujitsu*. *Gayong* and *silat* in general have many similarities to *jujitsu* including locks, throws, chokes, sweeps, and strikes. One thing *gayong* does stress in its training is to fight dirty. There are many arts that do not always get into this area of fighting. To survive a real street fight, you need to fight dirty. I'm not saying no other art trains in dirty fighting, but *gayong* actually has it in its training curriculum.

*Gayong* also has very unique training for weapons that we don't often see here in the United States. These weapons include *pentas,* a pre-choreographed fight with weapons. Not only do you learn to use the weapon, but also you slowly overcome the fear of the weapon by actually fighting with it.

My *gayong* teacher *Cikgu* Sheikh Shamsuddin always has us train with real weapons—live blades. This is an uncommon practice in the United States. At first I was very nervous, but because of the practice, my confidence has built up in weapons training.

You can learn both fear and respect for the weapon and still be confident in your defense against an opponent. When I go to visit other schools and see them train with wooden knives, I can't help but laugh inside.

I want to say thank you to my teacher *Cikgu* Sam for taking me on as his student in *silat seni gayong.* Not only is he a very good teacher, but he has also shown me how to look at my previous training in other arts in a different way.

Both *Cikgu* Sam and *gayong* have taught me not just the physical way of fighting, but how to approach combat mentally as well. Thank you.

# Gayong in the Eyes of Jennifer Para

I was first introduced to *silat seni gayong* by two of my friends who expressed excitement in the martial arts class they had taken earlier in the day. I was told to punch, and soon my arm was locked behind my back in a terribly uncomfortable position and my face was buried in the sidewalk. I was hooked. It was quick and effective, not to mention painful. The following week, I joined the class and have been with *gayong* ever since.

**Figure 18-3**

Training in this art for me is especially beneficial because of the fluidity of teaching. My teacher always reminds us to adjust, adjust to your surroundings, adjust to your opponent's size, and adjust to your opponent's fighting style. For a woman, this idea of adjusting is especially important; a woman needs to be aware of what she can do to be an effective fighter. I train in a predominantly male class and because of this I have to consistently modify and adjust what I do to fit the person with whom I am training. *Gayong's* variety of both weapons and open-hand techniques make it ideal for women.

*Silat seni gayong,* the Malaysian art of self-defense, combines functionality with versatility of form. *Gayong* is an intense martial art that combines hard and soft techniques for maximum damage. From a self-defense point of view, *Gayong* is very effective. If someone attacks with a fist or a weapon, we learn to evade the strike and then to quickly and efficiently end the fight. I am very lucky to have stumbled upon this art and grateful for the knowledge that I have been given. I look forward to continuing training in *silat seni gayong*.

CHAPTER *19*

# Names of Gayong Techniques

## *Buah Tapak* (**Fruit Techniques**)

The following list includes the names of twenty-one fruit techniques sometimes called body lock techniques. In Malay, these techniques are called *buah tapak* or sometimes, *tangkapan*.

The name translation from Malay to English has never been made before. The precise translation may not be possible to define, but below is the closest translation I consider appropriate.

1. *Ular Sawa Berendam*—Sinking Python

2. *Kilas Payong*—Twisting Umbrella

3. *Sangga Maut*—Deadly Support

4. *Kacip Emas*—Golden Slicer

5. *Patah Dayong*—Broken Paddle

6. *Cekak Banting*—Choking Throw

7. *Kacip Selak Emas*—Golden Locked Slicer

8. *Pasung Cina*—Chinese Vase

9. *Tali Gantong*—Hanging Rope

10. *Kilas Payong Tali Gantong*—Twisting Umbrella
Hanging Rope

11. *Selak Mati*—Dead Locked

12. *Kilas Tali*—Twisting Rope

13. *Tolak Lintang*—Horizontal Push

14. *Sekapur Sireh*—Friendly Gift

15. *Patah Layar Perahu Karam*—Broken Sail Sinking Boat

16. *Patah Julang*—Broken Boost

17. *Pangkah Sangga*—Cross Support

18. *Kilas Biawak*—Twisting Lizard

19. *Sangga Kilas Patah Tebu*—Twisting Support
                                        Broken Cane

20. *Pasak Mati*—Deadly Anchor

21. *Kilas Buaya Berendam*—Twisting Sinking Crocodile

## *Serangan Maut* (Super Combat)

The following list includes the names of twenty-one super combat techniques sometimes called tiger attack techniques. In Malay, these techniques are called *serangan maut* or *serangan harimau* or simply refer to as *kombat*.

The name translation from Malay to English has never been made before. The precise translation may not be possible to define, but below is the closest translation I consider appropriate.

1. *Patah Dayong Nasi Hangit*
   Broken Paddle Overcooked Rice

2. *Patah Dayong Kuda Gila*
   Broken Paddle Crazy Horse

3. *Kuda Gila*
   Crazy Horse

4. *Humban Ketan Kawah Pecah*
   Slamming Broken Crater

5. *Kipas Dayong Selak Gayong*
   Locking Fanning Paddle

6. *Pangku Mayat Pecah Kawah Hentak Kawah*
   Slamming Crater Supporting Corpse

7. *Kipas Gayong Tembi Gayong Selak Gayong*
   Fanning Locked Elbow

8. *Tembi Gayong Pasak Gayong Selak Gayong*
   Anchoring Locked Elbow

9. *Lipat Gayong Pangku Kawah Pecah Kawah*
   Cross Support Broken Crater

10. *Kawah Sepit Pecah Tebu*
    Pinning Crater Broken Cane

11. *Timang Putri Kawah Tiarap*
    Winding Princess Falling Crater

12. *Tembi Kilas Pangku Mayat Kawah Pecah*
    Twisting Elbow Supporting Corpse

13. *Gasing Emas*
    Golden Spin

14. *Pangku Lutut Patah Tebu*
    Supporting Knee Broken Cane

15. *Patah Halu Pangku Mayat*
    Broken Path Supporting Corpse

16. *Gasing Emas Kuda Gila Pangku Mayat*
    Golden Spin Crazy Horse Supporting Corpse

17. *Pikul Kawah Buang Kawah*
    Carrying Throwing Crater

18. *Buah Sepukai Selayang Pandang Selak Dayong Kuda Gila*
    Breezy Sight Crazy Horse Lock

19. *Buah Sepukai Siku Temi Simbat Relang Hentak Hadam*
    Stormy Elbow Sweeping Crater

20. *Buah Sepukai Siku Temi Patah Dayong Selak Mati*
    Stormy Elbow Broken Paddle Deadly Locked

21. *Tarian Kuda Gila*
    Crazy Horse Dance

CHAPTER 20

# Who Was Hang Tuah?

Malays consider Hang Tuah, who lived during the golden era of the Malacca Sultanate in the fifteenth century, as a legendary Malay warrior and the father of Malay *silat*. He represents the ultimate victor of Malay loyalty, courtesy, and obedience to tradition. Hang Tuah symbolizes the prominence of *Malacca* and projects the bravery of the Malays. His legend left us with an epic story filled with enigma.

Hang Tuah was a humble man and a great warrior. His diplomatic, linguistic, and fighting skills earned him the highest position in the Sultan's palace. He grew up with four of his dearest friends, Hang Jebat, Hang Lekir, Hang Lekiu, and Hang Kasturi—the five musketeers of Malay history. They considered themselves to be blood brothers. They mastered Malay *silat* and its mystical power. Some believe they received the art from the guru of Gunong Ledang (Ledang Mountain) in the state of Johor who also taught them mystic incantations and magic charms. Of the five brothers, Hang Tuah was considered the most skilled fighter. Their life was full of adventures. Hang Tuah's bravery was discovered during his adolescence when he single-handedly detained a man who had ran amok in the village Kampong Duyong. His heroic act caught the Sultan's attention, and Hang Tuah was called to the palace and bestowed knighthoods. He was the youngest ever to be knighted.

Legend has it that one day during the marriage ceremony of Sultan Mansur Shah of the Malacca Empire and the daughter of the Majapahit Emperor, Hang Tuah was insulted. A warrior from the Majapahit saw that Hang Tuah could dance but that he could not defend himself. With permission from the Sultan, they engaged in battle. In the fight, Hang Tuah was able to snatch his opponent's weapon, the legendary *keris* Taming Sari. Ultimately, Hang Tuah overpowered his challenger and kept the *keris* for himself. This *keris* was believed to have magical powers. Any person in possession of this weapon became impenetrable and able to impose lethal wounds upon enemies.

Hang Tuah was extremely loyal to the ruler. Responsibilities given to him were fulfilled without question. He was made the *laksamana* (admiral) and defended effectively countless attacks against Malacca sovereignty from Siamese and Achenese fleets. His outstanding performance as a military officer made him a legend that has refined the history of Malacca. He was held in such high esteem by the Sultan that his influence extended to many critical issues from politics to strategic interests. It guaranteed him the security of wealth and comfort. Unfortunately, it is occasionally true that no good deed goes unpunished. Many highly ambitious officials of the palace wanted to see him exiled. Hang Tuah was slandered by his enemies, who accused him of having an affair with the favorite concubine of the Sultan. The Sultan ordered him to be put to death. Hang Jebat and his closest friends pleaded for his life, but to no avail. He was executed.

With the absence of Hang Tuah, Hang Jebat became the newly appointed *laksamana*. At the same time, he was infuriated over the fact that his dearest friend had been put to death for a crime he did not commit. All the good deeds that he had done for the Sultan were disregarded. As a result, he ran amok and started killing the palace's

**Figure 20-1**

protectors and others who dared to challenge him. He stormed the Sultan's palace, driving everyone into hiding including the Sultan himself. In old Malay culture, this was considered *derhaka* (treason) and was punishable by death. With the *Taming Sari* in his hand, no one could defeat Hang Jebat as he was strong and invincible. The Sultan then regretted his hasty decision in ordering the execution of Hang Tuah.

What Hang Jebat and the Sultan did not know was that the *dato bendahara* (prime minister), who believed that Hang Tuah was innocent, had secretly spared Hang Tuah's life. The Sultan was thrilled to hear the news and fully pardoned Hang Tuah and sent him to meet Hang Jebat. Jebat was stunned, but overjoyed to see him alive. He was distressed to learn that Tuah, his precious friend whose death he had avenged, had been sent to take his life. According to legend, the only way to kill Jebat was to retrieve the *Taming Sari*. And so, the battle began.

In the dual, Tuah tried to snatch the *Taming Sari* from Jebat. Tuah twice dropped his own *keris,* but Jebat allowed him to pick it up and continue the dual. During the dual, each exchanged *pantun* (poems) questioning each other's ethics and loyalty. Jebat attempted to convince Tuah to disregard the past and take over the empire. Tuah ignored Jebat's idea and effectively snatched the *Taming Sari* from

him. Legend has it that the dual of honor was fought twice to a standstill and had to take a rest. In the subsequent clash, Jebat was killed. But at the end of his life, he still declared his loyalty to his dear friend. Tuah grieved over his dying friend. Jebat died in the trembling arms of Tuah. Hang Tuah himself was uncertain about what had occurred. Who was right? Was he supposed to remain loyal to the ruler or kill a traitor who fought injustice in defense of a dear friend? Tuah was upset about what he has done and vowed never to show himself again on the face of the earth. He vanished. Until this day no one knows where he went and his body was never found.

Except for Hang Jebat, Hang Kasturi, and the others remained loyal to the Sultan to their dying day.

**Figure 20-2**

There are two famous quotes taken from this legend. One came from Hang Tuah, and the other from Hang Jebat respectively:

*Takkan melayu hilang di dunia*—Malay race, culture, tradition, and language shall not perish from this earth.

*Raja adil raja disembah, raja zalim raja disanggah*—A just king is a king obeyed, a cruel king is a king defied.

Figure 20-2 on the left shows a manuscript relating the story of Hang Tuah. The manuscript is currently preserved in the National Library of Malaysia. The manuscript was written about 200 years ago. To this day, the author remains unknown.

The image on figure 20-3 shows Hang Tuah's symbolic mausoleum, and on figure 20-4 is Hang Jebat mausoleum. Both are located in the state of Melaka in Malaysia.

**Figure 20-3**                                    **Figure 20-4**

The King and Queen of Malaysia, Tuanku Syed Sirajuddin Al-Marhum Tuanku Syed Putra Jamalullail and Tuanku Fauziah Al-Marhum Tengku Abdul Rashid.

# CHAPTER 21

# To Know Malaysia

Malaysia, located in Southeast Asia, consists of two separate parts. They are Peninsular Malaysia and the two states of Sabah and Sarawak, found on the island of Borneo. Malaysia currently is comprised of thirteen states and the Federal Territories of Kuala Lumpur, the capital city. The population of Malaysia is approximately twenty-one million people, consisting of three major ethnic groups: Malay, Chinese, and Indian, as well as several other minority ethnic groups. The national language is Bahasa Malaysia. English is also widely spoken. Islam is the official religion, but other religions are practiced freely.

Malaysia is a tropical rain forest with temperatures ranging from seventy-five to ninety degrees fahrenheit year round. The days are pleasantly warm while the nights are cool.

The National flag, also known as *Jalur Gemilang* (Stripes of Glory) consists of fourteen red and blue stripes, which represent the states. The star symbolizes the unity of the people and the crescent symbol-

---

Most pictures in this section are courtesy of Tourism Malaysia Organization in New York, United States.

izes Islam as the official religion. The color yellow signifies the royal ruling color. Malaysia achieved its independence from British colonization on August 31, 1957. The current government is a constitutional monarchy with the prime minister as the governing power. With the inclusion of the states of Sabah and Sarawak, and the exclusion of Singapore and Brunei, Malaysia was formed on September 16, 1963 with the national anthem titled Negaraku (My Country).

The national flower of Malaysia is *bunga raya* (hibiscus). It was chosen because it is found in abundance throughout the country. The five petals symbolize the *rukun negara* (five principles of nationhood) and the color red represents courage. The flower is believed to have medicinal properties. The roots of the plant are used to cure fevers and other ailments, and the juice obtained from the leaves is said to be effective in relieving skin irritations and glandular troubles. The declaration of *rukun negara* is:

- Achieving a greater unity for all people.

- Maintaining a democratic way of life.

- Creating a just society in which the wealth of the nation shall be equally distributed.

- Ensuring a liberal approach to her rich and diverse cultural traditions.

- Building a progressive society, which shall be oriented towards modern science and technology.

The coat of arms of Malaysia includes basic elements such as the crest, the shield, and the motto *Bersekutu Bertambah Mutu* (Unity is Strength). The five *keris* represent the former unfederated Malay states of Johor, Kedah, Kelantan, Perlis, and Terengganu that joined the Federation in 1948.

Malaysia is a place where you can relax and enjoy the warm hospitality of its people. The country is rich in colorful cultures with diverse ethnic groups. With its wealth of natural environment, Malaysia offers plenty of adventure opportunities such as cave exploration, jungle trekking, scuba diving, white-water rafting, mountain and rock climbing, kayaking, and more. Throughout the country, the surroundings offer ideal activities—dense adventure forests, giant cave systems, rapid rivers, rugged mountains, rich

**Orang Iban dance.**

**Ubudiah Mosque in Kuala Kangsar.**

wildlife, and prehistoric indigenous peoples. In the state of Perlis, you will find unspoiled beauty and vast paddy fields. Kedah is considered the "rice bowl of Malaysia," and contains the gorgeous Langkawi island. Penang state is known as the "pearl of the Orient." Perak is known for its cave temple and beautiful foliage. The state is rich with tin deposits. Selangor is the most prosperous state and is considered "the heart of modern Malaysia." Negeri Sembilan is known for its *Minangkabau* influence. Malacca the "historical city of Malaysia," has Portuguese, Dutch, and British influences. Johor is known for its attractive offshore islands. Pahang hosts the beautiful national park, Taman Negara, lovingly referred as "the green heart." Terengganu is known

**City of Kuala Lumpur (KL).**

**Replica of the king's palace of Negeri Sembilan state.**

for its magical beaches, clear water, and boating activities. Kelantan is the "cradle of Malaysian culture." Sarawak is known for its majestic mountains and caves, and its diverse ethnic groups. Sabah is the "land below the wind," with natural flora and fauna and the world's largest orangutan rehabilitation center. Kuala Lumpur, also known as KL, is the capital of Malaysia—the "modern city." This is the largest city in the nation with modern components. Putrajaya is the cyber-province of the future government administrative center. Malaysia gives ample opportunities to discover nature and enjoy its contemporary amenities. Those who have visited Malaysia sum up the country as "exciting, fascinating, and mystifying."

In 1984, Grammy and Academy Award winning lyricist and songwriter Carol Conners from Beverly Hills, California, visited Malaysia and was so fascinated by the country and its people that she wrote a

**Sultan Abdul Samad Building.**

beautiful song to express her feelings for the country, "To Know Malaysia is to Love Malaysia."

*To know Malaysia is to love Malaysia.*

*People smiling everywhere, showing you how much they care.*

*To know Malaysia is to love Malaysia. It's true.*

*This land's so beautiful. It will steal your heart away.*

*This land is paradise. And it's only, only a smile away.*

*To know Malaysia is to love Malaysia.*

*In this land where dreams come true. Malaysia welcomes you.*

*To know Malaysia is to love Malaysia.*

*It's true, it's true, it's true.*

**Decorating floating boat.**

**Malaysia International Kite Festival.**

Rabana Ubi

Malay dance.

Typical Malaysian *kampong* (village).

**Typical Malaysian *kampong*.**

# CHAPTER 22

# Mahaguru Message (Amanat Mahaguru)

*Tiang yang paling penting dalam tuntutan ilmu ialah taat setia yang tidak berbelah bagi. Tamak ahmak itu adalah satu daripada membunuh diri sendiri ataupun satu kecelakaan kepada diri seseorang itu.*

The most treasured possession in gathering knowledge is honesty and loyalty. Greediness is a quality that will ultimately demolish oneself.

**Figure 22-1**

> *Seni Gayong Payung Pusaka*
> *Naungan Aneka Hikmat Mulia*
> *Rahsia Tersimpan Di Purbakala*
> *Ilham Menyusur Zahir Semula*
>
> *The Art of Gayong, The Canopy of Heritage*
> *The Patron of Wisdoms, Various and Virtuous*
> *Secrets Once Kept in Days of Old*
> *Now Reborn of Vision Retold★*

---

★The poem was translated to English by Mohd Nadzrin Wahab from Malaysia

# CHAPTER 23

# Collection of Gayong Pictures and Events

A. *Cikgu* Ariffin being endorsed by *Cikgu* Razali to represent *gayong* in United Kingdom

B. *Cikgu* Ibrahim receiving 6th *dan* black belt

C. *Gayong* demo using long sticks

D. *Gayong* student receiving 3rd *dan* yellow belt

E. *Cikgu* Razali giving sash titled *Khalifah* to *gayong* student

F. *Gayong* student receiving 3rd *dan* black belt

G. *Gayong* demo using machete

Fig 23-1

Some pictures in this section are courtesy of *Seni Beladiri* magazine and Malaysian *gayong* Web sites.

Breaking a coconut with bare hand.

*Harimau mengambur* (tiger jump).

Forward leap roll.

Bending hot metal with teeth.

A *gayong* training center in Malaysia.

A *gayong* training center in Malaysia.

*Gayong* machete demo in Malaysia.

*Cikgu* Rasol and his students.

The author and his students in suburban Chicago.

*Cikgu* Kahar, *Cikgu* Jazwan, and United Kingdom students visiting Malaysia.

*Cikgu* Amin Hamzah, chief instructor of *gayong* in Darul Ridzuan province in the state of Perak.

Bending metal using his neck.

Breaking a huge tile on top of a student's chest.

Peeling a coconut with his teeth at a *gayong pedana* (demo) in Malaysia, 2001.

Demo on car going over
*Cikgu* Amin's arm.

After marching on Independence Day, August 31, 1978.

Culture sharing—*gayong* plays a role in the ASEAN
summit meeting in 1978.

*Cikgu* Joel Champ and his brother Joshua Champ in action.

*Gayong* acrobatics.

Students visiting the *Daeing Kuning*, also known the as *Panglima Hitam* (Black Warrior) cemetery in Malaysia.

*Dato* Meor with his medal of honor.

*Gayong* demo using machete—Multimedia University in Malaysia.

*Gayong* demo using long sticks—Multimedia University in Malaysia.

*Gayong* demo—Multimedia University in Malaysia.

Breaking tiles.

Students from the United Kingdom in action.

*Gayong pendekar* seminar in Tapah, Perak, Malaysia.

Machete demo in Malaysia.

Hot oil bath.

Posing after *gayong* demo.

Breaking tiles.

*Gurulatih* Colin Shahley from the United Kingdom with *Cikgu* Azhar Abbas.

*Cikgu* Kahar Redza, Kuala Lumpur, Malaysia.

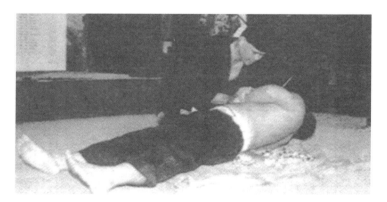

Demonstrator rolls his body over broken glass.

Tok Jenai training center, Pahang, Malaysia. Picture by Zazri Abdullah taken from *Seni Beladiri* magazine.

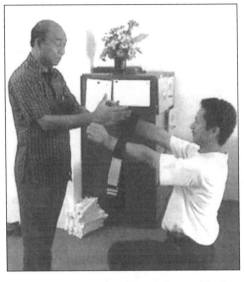

The author receiving second degree black belt from *Cikgu* Razali Salleh in 1999.

*Cikgu* Sulaiman Shariff and Blaise Loong.

*Cikgu* Mufti with his students in France.

*Cikgu* Zainal Ishak receiving his sixth degree black belt.

Slashing on student's back with iron rod and walking on hot charcoal.

*Cikgu* Awang Daud in action.

*Cikgu* Amin receiving his black belt from *Dato* Meor.

*Cikgu* Ahmad Lazim doing a flying kick.

Demo on breaking bricks.

Hajjah Fatimah (*Cikgu* Awang's wife) showing *gayong* technique.

Confidence test on *gayong* students in Malaysia.

At University of Malaya in 1977, *gayong* demo using machete. The author (right), *Cikgu* Faid (left), and *Cikgu* Rasol (on ground).

*Cikgu* Ismail Jantan, senior instructor in Melaka state.

*Gayong* demo in Naperville, IL, USA, May 13, 2004.

*Cikgu* Sani Morni, one of senior instructors in KL.

*Gayong* demo in Naperville, May 13, 2004.

*Cikgu* Ariffin and his students in the United Kingdom.

**Machete training course in Kuala Lumpur, Malaysia.**

*Gayong* **seminar in 1997 in Downers Grove, IL.**

*Cikgu* **Nordin Rahman, senior**
*gayong* **instructor in the state**
**of Perlis.**

# CHAPTER 24

# Conclusion

I hope this book serves its purpose and offers an introduction and understanding of *seni gayong silat*. The techniques illustrated in this book are only a fraction of the art. Some techniques are difficult or impossible to put in a still picture due to the nature of movement. Based on the basic replica techniques in each category, hundreds or even thousands of other variation techniques can be applied. Once you have mastered the essential keys, roots, and principles, you will be able to develop and grow continuously with no limits.

Allow me to remind you that when you practice, please take every measure to prevent injury from occurring. Life and health are too precious to chance. Always practice with care for you and for your partner.

Self-defense is not purely with reference to strength and physical movement or techniques. There are other aspects of self-defense that we all should consider such as verbal and psychological skills to pre-empt violent attacks, threat recognition to keep danger at a distance, and self-preservation. I believe that the real victory is the fight that needs never be fought. This ought to be the ultimate goal for all martial art practitioners. Remain humble and kind-hearted.

Finally, allow me to leave you with the following words. Those who query gain. Those who seek discover, and those who learn prevail. To truly understand the fighting aspect of *silat* one requires patience and dedication, and most importantly a master that can teach and guide. Memorizing all techniques alone is not enough. Repetition is the key to skillfully executing techniques and building confidence and self-control. Practice, practice, practice.

May you find what your journey brings. Peace be upon you. *Salaam.*

# APPENDIX A:
## United States *Gayong* Federation Syllabus Requirements

### *Pelangi putih*—white belt (60 hours)

- *Asas gerakkan* one and two—basic movements one and two
- *Asas elakkan* one and two—basic blocks one and two
- *Gulungan* 10—ten steps preset movement
- *Tarian bunga tanjung*—bay flower dance
- *Serangan maut* one through four—super combat one through four
- *Buah tapak kunci mati* one through four—grappling and takedown, dead-lock techniques one through four
- *Pecahan buah tapak kunci mati dan kombat*—breakdown/variation of dead-lock techniques and super combat
- *Pentas* I—counter attack one
- *Tengelling dan lompatan*—basic gymnastics
- *Lompatan harimau mengambur*—forward roll over an obstacle
- *Lepasan dari gengaman*—escape from hand grappling and joint locks
- *Serangan bebas*—free sparring

### *Pelangi hijau*—green belt (60 hours)
(Hour requirements are counted from the last test)

- *Asas gerakkan three*—basic movement three
- *Asas elakkan three*—basic blocks three
- *Gulungan* 21—twenty-one steps preset movement

- *Serangan maut* one through eight—super combat one through eight
- *Buah tapak kunci mati/tangkapan* one through eight—Grappling and takedown, dead-lock techniques one through eight
- *Pecahan buah tapak kunci mati dan kombat*—Breakdown/variation of dead-lock techniques and super combat
- *Pentas II*—Counter attack two
- *Lompatan harimau mengambur; tambahan*—forward roll over an obstacle; additional
- *Lompatan pagar dan lompatan dahan*—forward roll over a fence and an obstacle
- *Lepasan dari gengaman; tambahan*—escape from hand grappling and joint locks; additional
- *Serangan bebas*—free sparring and defense on multiple attacks

## Pelangi merah—red belt (60 hours)

- *Asas gerakkan four*—basic movement four
- *Asas elakkan four*—basic blocks four
- *Gulungan 31*—thirty-one steps preset movement
- *Serangan maut* one through twelve—super combat one through twelve
- *Buah tapak kunci mati/tangkapan* one through twelve—grappling and takedown, dead-lock techniques one through twelve
- *Pecahan buah tapak kunci mati dan kombat*—breakdown/variation of body dead-lock fruit and super combat
- *Pentas III*—counter attack three

- *Lompatan harimau mengambur; tambahan*—forward roll over an obstacle; additional
- *Lompatan gelung*—forward roll through a hula hoop
- *Lepasan dari gengaman; tambahan*—escape from hand grappling and joint locks; additional
- *Serangan bebas; tambahan*—free sparring and defense on multiple attacks; additional
- *Asas pisau—basic knife usage*
- *Gulungan 21 pisau*—twenty-one steps knife preset movement

## *Pelangi merah cula I hingga III*—red belt stripe one through three (48 hours each stripe)

- *Asas gerakkan* five—basic movement five
- *Asas elakkan* five—basic blocks five
- *Gulungan 49*—forty-nine steps preset movement
- *Serangan maut* one through sixteen—super combat one through sixteen
- *Buah tapak kunci mati/tangkapan one* through sixteen—grappling and takedown, dead-lock techniques one through sixteen
- *Pecahan buah tapak kunci mati dan kombat*—breakdown/variation of dead-lock techniques and super combat
- *Pukulan* one through seven—striking one through seven
- *Pentas IV*—counter attack four
- *Lompatan harimau mengambur; tambahan*—forward roll over an obstacle; additional

- *Lompatan gelung; tambahan*—forward roll through a hula hoop; additional

- *Asas pisau*—basic knife

- *Serangan bebas; tambahan*—free sparring and defense on multiple attacks; additional

- *Lepasan dari gengaman; tambahan*—escape from hand grappling and joint locks; additional

## *Pelangi merah cula II*—red belt stripe two

- *Asas gerakkan* six—basic movement six

- *Asas elakkan* six—basic blocks six

- *Serangan maut* one through twenty-one—super combat one through twenty-one

- *Buah tapak kunci mati/tangkapan* one through twenty-one—grappling and takedown, dead-lock techniques one-twenty

- *Pecahan buah tapak kunci mati dan kombat*—breakdown/variation of dead-lock techniques and super combat

- *Pentas V*—counter attack five

- *Pukulan* one through fourteen—body strike—one through fourteen

- *Asas simbat*—basic short staff

- *Serangan bebas*—free sparring and defense on multiple attacks; additional

- *Lepasan dari gengaman; tambahan*—escape from hand grappling and joint locks; additional

## *Pelangi merah cula III*—red belt stripe three

- *Asas gerakkan seven*—basic movement seven
- *Asas elakkan seven*—basic blocks seven
- *Pecahan buah tapak kunci mati dan kombat*—breakdown/variation of dead-lock techniques and super combat
- *Pentas VI and VII*—counter attack six and seven
- *Pukulan* one through twenty-one—striking –one through twenty-one
- *Asas kayu panjang*—basic long stick
- *Serangan bebas; tambahan*—free sparing and defense on multiple attacks; additional
- *Lepasan dari gengaman; tambahan tambahan*—escape from hand grappling and joint locks, additional

## *Pelangi kuning cula I hingga V*—yellow belt stripe one through five) (96 hours each stripe)

- *Seni pisau; tambahan*—the art of knife; additional
- *Seni tongkat panjang*—the art of long stick
- *Seni simbat*—the art of short staff
- *Seni parang panjang*—the art of machete
- *Seni keris*—the art of dagger
- *Seni lembing/tombak*—the art of spear

### *Pelangi hitam cula I hingga VI*—black belt stripe one through six (96 hours each stripe)

- *Seni yoi*—the art of deception

- *Seni belian*—the art of tearing and internal strength

- *Seni cindai; sauk-sauk, tebar, serkap, kain tudung, awang bodoh, pukat, kalung puteri*—the art of rope, chain, cloth, belt, vail

- *Seni sundang lipas*—the art of a *bugis* weapon (similar to a Viking sword)

- *Seni seligi*

- *Additional syllabus*

    *Senjata api*—handgun disarmament

    *Lawi ayam (kerambit, a knife-shaped-like a tiger claw)*

    *Tekpi (sai)*

    *Pedang*—sword

    *Seni selayang pandang*

    *Seni serangan rajawali*

    *Gerak bayang*

    *Serbuk beracun*

    *Mayang gesit*

- Attending seminars

# APPENDIX B:
## How to Count in Malay

The following shows how to count in the Malay language from one to thirty-one. The pronunciation presented is American English. The count is also similar to Indonesian language. Malay language is spoken in Malaysia as well as in Indonesia. In Malaysia, the language is called *Bahasa Malaysia,* and in Indonesia the language is called *Bahasa Indonesia.*

1. **Satu** (sah tu)—One

2. **Dua** (do wah)—Two

3. **Tiga** (tee gah)—Three

4. **Empat** (em pot)—Four

5. **Lima** (li mah)—Five

6. **Enam** (a nam)—Six

7. **Tujuh** (tu joe)—Seven

8. **Lapan** (la pahn)—Eight

9. **Sembilan** (sem be lahn)—Nine

10. **Sepuluh** (suh poo low)—Ten

11. **Sebelas** (suh blass)—Eleven

12. **Duabelas** (do wah blass)—Twelve

13. **Tigabelas** (tee gah blass)—Thirteen

14. **Empatbelas** (em pot blass)—Fourteen

15. **Limabelas** (li mah blass)—Fifteen

16.  **Enambelas** (a num blass)—Sixteen

17.  **Tujuhbelas** (to joe blass)—Seventeen

18.  **Lapanbelas** (la phan blass)—Eighteen

19.  **Sembilanbelas** (sem be lahn blass)—Nineteen

20.  **Duapuluh** (do wah poo low)—Twenty

21.  **Duapuluh satu** (do wah poo low sa tu)—Twenty-one

22.  **Duapulih dua** (do wah poo low do wah)—Twenty-two

23.  **Duapuluh tiga** (do wah poo low tee gah)—Twenty-three

24.  **Duapuluh empat** (do wah poo low em pot)—Twenty-four

25.  **Duapuluh lima** (do wah poo low li mah)—Twenty-five

26.  **Duapuluh enam** (do wah poo low a nam)—Twenty-six

27.  **Duapuluh tujuh** (do wah poo low tu joe)—Twenty-seven

28.  **Duapuluh lapan** (do wah poo low la phan)—Twenty-eight

29.  **Duapuluh sembilan** (do wah poo low sem be lahn)—Twenty-nine

30.  **Tigapuluh** (tee gah poo low)—Thirty

31.  **Tigapuluh satu** (tee gah poo low sa tu)—Thirty-one

# APPENDIX C:
## Glossary

**Adat**—Culture, laws of conduct

**Ahli**—Member

**Angkat**—Lift

**Asas**—Basic

**Bahu**—Shoulder

**Bapak**—Father

**Batin**—Spiritual, within the heart

**Beladiri**—Self-defense

**Belajar**—Learn

**Bengkong**—Belt

**Berlatih**—Practicing

**Buah**—Fruit. In *silat* terms, it refers to a *silat* technique.

**Buka**—Open

**Bunga**—Flower. Also refers to *silat* dance.

**Cikgu, Guru**—Teacher

**Duduk**—Sit

**Elak, tepis**—Avoidance

**Elak makan**—Block and counter

**Gelanggang**—Training dojo

**Genggam**—Full fist

**Harimau, macan**—Tiger

**Humban, banting**—Throw

**Jurus, djurus**—Short form or movement

**Kampong**—Village

**Kaki**—Leg

**Khalifah**—*Caliph* or leader of a group

**Kawan, sahabat**—Friend

**Kepala**—Head

**Kerambit, Lawi Ayam**—Tiger-claw weapon

**Kibas, sapu**—Sweep kick

**Kuda Kuda**—Horse stance

**Kunci**—Lock

**Tangan kosong**—Empty-handed

**Langkah**—Steps

**Latihan**—Practice

**Lawan bebas**—Free sparring

**Leher**—Neck

**Lembing**—Spear

**Libas**—Swing

**Lompat**—Jump

**Mahaguru**—Grand Master

**Makan**—Eat

**Mandi**—Bath

**Mata**—Eyes

**Mati**—Die

**Melayu**—Malay people

**Muka**—Face

**Murid**—Student

**Naga**—Dragon

**Pancung, tetak**—Strike or chop

**Parang**—Machete

**Pecah**—Break, broken

**Pedang**—Sword

**Pelajaran**—Syllabus

**Pernafasan**—Breathing

**Pertubuhan**—Organization

**Pertunjukkan**—Demonstration

**Pisau**—Knife

**Pulas**—Twisting

**Rahsia**—Secret

**Raja, Sultan**—King

**Sarong**—Cloth

**Saya**—I, myself

**Selamat**—Safe, with respect, a greeting

**Selempang**—Sash

**Senaman**—Exercise

**Sejarah**—History

**Serang**—Attack

**Siku**—Elbow

**Simbat**—Short stick about three to four feet long

**Sri Kandi**—Title given to a *gayong* female practitioner

**Olahraga**—*Silat* sport competition

**Tangan**—Hand

**Tangkap**—Catch

**Tangkis**—Block

**Tarik**—Pull

**Tenaga dalam**—Internal energy

**Tendang depan**—Front kick

**Tendang juring**—Side kick

**Tendang layang**—Roundhouse kick

**Tendang, sepak, terajang**—Kick

**Tikam**—Thrusting

**Tolak**—Push

**Tumbuk**—Punch

**Tumbuk kun**—Upper-cut punch

**Tutup**—Close

**Ujian**—Test

**Waris**—Heritage

**Zahir dan Batin**—External and internal

**Zikir**—Quietly uttering Almighty word repeatedly, a mantra

# APPENDIX D:
## Malay Language Helper

## First Things

Yes—*Ya*

No—*Tidak*

Please—*Tolong*

Thank you—*Terima kasih*

You're welcome—*Sama sama*

Sorry—*Maaf*

My name is—*Nama saya*

What is your name?—*Siapa nama awak?*

## Language problems

Do you speak English?—*Awak cakap English?*

Do you understand me?—*Awak faham cakap saya?*

Please speak slowly.—*Tolong cakap pelahan sedikit.*

I don't understand.—*Saya tidak faham.*

What does it mean?—*Apa maknanya?*

When—*Bila*

Who—*Siapa*

Why—*Kenapa*

What—*Apa*

Enough—*Cukup*

How much does it cost?—*Berapa harga?*

How far—*Berapa jauh?*

I want—*Saya mahu*

Can you help me?—*Boleh tolong saya?*

Can you show me?—*Boleh tolong tunjukkan saya?*

Can you tell me?—*Boleh tolong beritahu saya?*

## Useful statements

I don't like it.—*Saya tidak suka.*

I'm not sure.—*Saya tidak pasti.*

I don't know.—*Saya tidak tahu.*

I think so.—*Saya fikir begitu.*

I'm hungry.—*Saya lapar.*

I'm thirsty.—*Saya dahaga.*

I'm tired.—*Saya penat.*

I'm ready.—*Saya sudah sedia.*

Leave me alone.—*Jangan ganggu saya.*

Just one minute.—*Tunggu sekejap.*

Please come in.—*Sila masuk.*

It is cheap?—*Murah?*

It is expensive?—*Mahal?*

It is cold?—*Sejuk?*

It is hot?—*Panas?*

That is all.—*Itu sahaja.*

Thank you for your help.—*Terima kasih pertolongan awak.*

Taxi please.—*Tolong panggil taxi.*

Sick—*Sakit*

# Greetings

Welcome—*Selamat datang*

Good morning.—*Selamat pagi.*

Good night.—*Selamat malam.*

Goodbye—*Selamat tinggal*

Hello—*Hi*

How are you?—*Apa khabar?*

Very well, thank you.—*Kabar baik, terima kasih.*

See you soon.—*Jumpa lagi.*

That is all right.—*Semua bagus saja.*

Don't worry.—*Jangan khuatir.*

# Opposites

Before / after—*Sebelum / selepas*

Early / Late—*Cepat / lambat*

First / last—*Pertama / akhir*

Here / there—*Sini / sana*

Now / then—*Sekarang / kemudian*

Large / small—*Besar / kecil*

Empty / full—*Kosong / penuh*

Many / few—*Banyak / sedikit*

Beautiful / ugly—*Cantik / hodoh*

Better / worse—*Bagus / tidak bagus*

Clean / dirty—*Bersih / kotor*

Cold / hot—*Sejuk / panas*

Free/taken—*Percuma/diambil*

Open/close—*Buka/tutup*

# ABOUT THE AUTHOR

Sheikh Shamsuddin (his full Malaysian name is Sheikh Shamsuddin bin Tan Sri Dato Sheikh Muhammad Salim), also known as Sam, is a Malaysian native who first learned *gayong* in Malaysia in early 1973. He is ranked *pelangi hitam harimau cula sakti* (fifth degree black belt) in the Gayong Malaysia hierarchy and carries the title *ketua khalifah* (chief of caliph). Shamsuddin started teaching *gayong* in Malaysia, and has taught the practice to many local high schools, colleges, and private training centers in Kuala Lumpur. He has also studied other martial arts, such as the Korean martial art *hapkido* and the Japanese art *aikido,* and has attended different martial art disciplines such as *kosho ryu kempo* and *kuntao silat.*

Shamsuddin is a member of Pentjak Silat USA and United States Aikido Federation, and has given several *silat* seminars with martial art practitioners in the United States such as Guru William De Thouars *(kuntao silat)* and Victor De Thouars *(serak silat),* Guru Jim Ingram *(mustika kuwitang silat),* Guru Dr. Andre KnutGraichen *(kuntao),* Guru Stevan Plinck *(serak),* Guru Wayne Welsh *(kuntao), hapkido* instructor master Randy Stigall, and Bruce Juchnik Hanshi *(kosho ryu kempo).* He has also given seminars with other Malaysian instructors such as *Cikgu* Majid Mat Isa, *Cikgu* Kahar, and *Cikgu* Ariffin Mahidin (Gayong United Kingdom).

Shamsuddin graduated from Bradley University in Peoria, Illinois, with a bachelor's degree in electrical engineering technology and a master's degree in computer science. He currently works as a system and network engineer at Lucent Technologies, Inc., a telecommunications company, and continues to teach *gayong* in suburban Chicago, where he lives with his wife, Melanie, and two daughters, Leila and Jasmine.

The picture on the right below shows the Shamsuddin and his brother, Sheikh Shamsul, being endorsed to propagate *silat seni gayong* in the United States by *Cikgu* Razali Salleh of Silat Seni Gayong Malaysia, accompanied by two of his assistants *Cikgu* Azhar Abbas on his right and *Cikgu* Rasol Abdul Ghani on his left. The picture on the left below shows Shamsuddin being endorsed by *Cikgu* Majid Mat Isa of Pusaka Gayong. Shamsuddin can be contacted at shamsudd@cdnet.cod.edu and *Cikgu* Joel Champ can be contacted at champjc3@aol.com.

The author being endorsed by *Cikgu* Majid Mat Isa to propagate *pusaka gayong*. *Cikgu* Majid visited New Jersey in 1998, invited by *Cikgu* Sulaiman Shariff.

The author being endorsed by *Cikgu* Razali Salleh to propagate *gayong* Malaysia in the U.S.

# RESOURCES

1. *Seni Beladiri* magazine, Jalur Citranusa (M) Sdn Bhd., Taman Setapak Indah, Kuala Lumpur, Malaysia

2. United States Gayong Federation, http://home.att.net/~gayong

3. P.S.S.G.M cawangan Tanjung Puteri, Johor Darul Takzim, http://www.geocities.com/Tokyo/Fuji/7899

4. P.S.S.G.M. SMAPL, http://members.tripod.com/gayongsmapl

5. P.S.S.G.M. USM (Kampus Cawangan Perak), http://members.tripod.com/gayongusmkcp77

6. P.S.S.G.M Kampus Kejuruturuan USM, http://www1.eng.usm.my/pssgm

7. P.S.S.G.M UPSI, http://www.pssgmupsi.8m.com

8. Gayong at University Malaya, http://members.tripod.com/~onnjadi/frame.html

9. P.S.S.G.M Daerah Kubang Pasu, Kedah Darul Aman, http://www.geocities.com/gayong_jitra

10. P.S.S.G.M UTM Kuala Lumpur, http://www.geocities.com/gayong_utmkl

11. Laman Sendomaster, http://www.geocities.com/sendomaster

12. Majlis Gurulatih Negeri Selangor/Wilayah Persekutuan, http://mgnswp.tripod.com

13. Pertubuhan Seni Silat Gayong Warisan Serantau Malaysia, http://members.tripod.com/gayong_warisan

14. Gayong Negeri Perlis Indera Kayangan, http://members.tripod.com/~indera_kayangan/index.html

15. P.S.S.G PASAK Melaka, http://www.geocities.com/ssgpasakmelaka/index.htm

16. Silat Association of the United Kingdom (GAYONG UK), http://www.silatassociation.co.uk

17. Gayong Universiti Sains Malaysia,
http://www1.eng.usm.my/pssgm/aktiviti/aktiviti.htm

18. Draeger, Donn F. and Smith, Robert W.: *Asian Fighting Arts.*
Tokyo: Kodansha, 1969

19. Draeger, Donn F.: *The Weapons and Fighting Arts of Indonesia.*
Charles T. Tuttle Company. Rutland, 1972

20. Wiley, Carol A.: *Martial Arts Teachers on Teaching.* Frog, Ltd.,
Berkeley, Calif., 1995

21. Frey, Edward: *The Kris: Mystic Weapon of the Malay World.*
Oxford University Press, New York, 2003

22. Ku Ahmad Bin Ku Mustaffa and Wong Kiew Kit: *SILAT
MELAYU, The Malay Art of Attack and Defence.* Oxford Press
University, Pertaling Jaya, Selangor, Malaysia, 1978

*Seni Beladiri* magazine about Malay *Silat*